GERALD;

A Dramatic Poem:

AND

OTHER POEMS.

BY

J. WESTLAND MARSTON,

AUTHOR OF " THE PATRICIAN'S DAUGHTER," A TRAGEDY.

" We are such stuff
As dreams are made of; and our little life
Is rounded with a sleep."

" Spirits are not finely touched
But to fine issues."

SHAKSPEARE

LONDON :

C. MITCHELL, RED LION COURT, FLEET STREET.

MDCCCXLII.

TO

CHARLES DICKENS, ESQ.

—◆—

My Dear Sir,

I inscribe to you the following pages as a very humble acknowledgment of many delightful hours, for which, in common with the public at large, I am indebted to your pen.

I would hope, too, that my obligations have not been restricted to the mere gratification derived from your works; but that I have been in some degree susceptible of their tendencies to foster generous feelings and benevolent sentiments. Indeed, the man who finds *mere* entertainment in an *imaginative* work, and whose sympathies are neither developed nor confirmed by its truth, pathos, and beauty—would probably peruse the *gravest moral treatise*, without gaining any practical benefit from his studies.

It is sometimes the good fortune of the grateful to evince their sense of favours by reciprocating them. But it frequently happens that a simple expression of their debt, is all that is permitted them. The latter method is the only one at my disposal, but I cannot too sincerely thank you for the privilege of using it.

Believe me to remain,

My dear Sir,

Your very faithful

And obliged Servant,

J. WESTLAND MARSTON.

London,
October, 1842.

PREFACE.

————

I HAD conceived the design of GERALD, and made some progress in its composition, in the Spring of 1841. My intention was, from such materials—whether dignified or humble—as the times presented, to construct a Poem of Dramatic—perhaps of Tragic—interest. The endeavour was, for the period, abandoned; not from any doubt of the legitimacy of the aim; but from a fear lest it should not be realized in a manner to satisfy the Author, and to interest the Public.

The cordial reception subsequently given to "The Patrician's Daughter," and the generous consideration afforded to it by the critical world—have, however, induced me to resume my labour, the result of which, is the principal poem in the following collection.

To choose the struggles and experiences of

Genius as a subject, might seem to evince temerity, if not presumption, on the part of the Author. But, were such a reflection allowed any weight, it would preclude the attempt to portray the heroic,—not only in the instance of the Poet—but in those of the Warrior, the Patriot, and the Philosopher. For what is the heroic in Man, but *his Genius?*

The Reader will bear in mind that all I have contemplated is the illumination of *certain points* in Gerald's mental history—to show the *crises* of his developements, not their *progress.*

I am aware that a nobler estimate of the Poetical character might have been given, than I have endeavoured to portray. The truly religious is the perfectly poetical ; and in accordance with this axiom I might have represented my Hero with motives as pure, as his purposes were great— subduing scepticism by the vitality of his devotion, disarming sarcasm by the benevolence of his nature, and overcoming trial by the constancy of his faith. Still the delineation of a great mind, subject to infirmities and swayed by passions, is not without peculiar advantages, too obvious to need specification.

Although I hope this work is in some measure

dramatic, I have not thought it necessary to adhere to the canons of the Drama, so strictly, as if the Poem had been intended for Theatrical representation. *Effects* have not been studied; nor, on the other hand, have they been avoided, when the progress of the story seemed naturally to admit of them.

J. W. M.

CONTENTS.

CHARACTERS OF THE POEM.

———◆———

EUSTACE LOVEL.

GERALD, *his Son.*

ASHTON, *a popular Man of Letters.*

CLAYTON, *an opulent London Merchant.*

LORD ROXMORE.

SIR HARRY BEVERLEY.

TOWNSMEN.

A VILLAGE PHYSICIAN.

FRANKLIN, *a Yeoman.*

A LONDON BEGGAR, *&c. &c.*

EDITH FAIRLIE, *Ward of* EUSTACE, *and betrothed to*
GERALD.

LADY ROXMORE.

MARGARET, *a Country Woman.*

LANDLADY.

LAURA, *a Child, &c. &c.*

*The Scene lies, partly, near a small Country Town;
and partly, in London.*

GERALD.

—

HOME.

GERALD.

HOME.

SCENE.—*A Garden by the Way-side.   A Country
Town in the Distance.*—TIME—*Evening.*

GERALD *and* EDITH.

GERALD.

Why art thou silent, Sweet?   To-morrow night
I shall not hear thy voice.

EDITH.

And know'st thou not
How oft the mournful heart restrains the tongue?
The feelings in their lone regality,
Wave language from their thrones.   I could believe—
I do not, but I could—thy glowing speech
Too eloquent for Love.

GERALD.

The Knight of old,
Vanished in gladness from his lady's bower,
His lip unfaltering, and his eye undimmed;
Yet, how he loved—

EDITH.

No!

GERALD.

More than tears had told.
The peril all was his; the fame, if won,

B 2

He shared with her; and to that soldier's eye
The Future was the Instant.—At her feet
Already lay the trophies of his lance,
The arms of Knights in tournay overthrown,
The gem plucked from the Misbeliever's brow,
The starry baldric, token from a Prince!
He thought not of the weary pilgrimage,
The scorching sun, more fatal than the sword;
The shadeless sands, amid whose arid waste
No fountain springs to quench the thirst of Death.

EDITH.
The thirst of Death! He died then; hapless Knight!

GERALD.
Nay, droop not; well I know that sigh had birth
In some foreboding of *thy* champion's fate.
Now smile;—methinks the Orient's in thy face.

EDITH.
Am I so changed since yester-eve? For then
I was your Phidian Goddess; you rejoiced
In what you thought the clear, pale purity;
No warmer tint profaned;—there's word for word.
Yet am I now your Oriental Nymph,
And the rich olive has suffused the cheek
So lately marble. Shall I tell you, love!
Your Eastern Girl to-night is paler far
Than was your last night's Goddess-statue? Well!
A Poet's fancy hath strange power to make
The thing it wills, and me it hath transformed
Oft as the year hath days. Have I not been
A Grecian Captive now—a Druidess
Anon—a Swiss Maid—nay, a Brigand's Wife—
Venus—Diana—Ceres?

GERALD.

Well, for change,
Thou shalt be Proserpine.

EDITH.

The Queen of Shades,
And Sorrows!

GERALD (*with sudden sadness*).

Truly, Edith! for thine own
Is such an Empire.

EDITH.

Mine!

GERALD.

My heart is thine.

EDITH (*weeping*).

You should not without need invoke these tears.

GERALD.

'Twas but a moment's mood, love! Nay, look up;
Bid but the sunlight pierce this crystal dew,
And I will call thee—Iris!

EDITH.

Ah! mine own!
There is a title that I covet more
Than any thou hast given me.

GERALD.

Name it, Sweet!

EDITH.

The simple one of—*Woman*.

GERALD.

All my thoughts
Tend to thee as a peerless work of Heaven;
Distinct, alone, apart. I'd have thee walk
Through earth as might an Angel clad in beams,

Fenced by thy very glory from the crowd
Whose sight thy presence blessed !

EDITH.

Oh, were I pure, and radiant as the host
That in the everlasting brightness dwell,
Methinks 'twould please me best to furl my wings,
To veil my glory, and in earthly guise
To seek the homes of men, as did of yore
The Patriarch's heavenly guests,—their nature learned
But by the blessing which they left behind.

GERALD.

What could excel thy human loveliness ?
What change—that would not mar it ? To these eyes,
Since they beheld thee, all of fair beside
Hath lost its proper life, to live in thine.
There's not a tree that bends above the stream,
But in its graceful curve thine outline dwells :
There's not a singing brook, but that I deem
Thee vocal in its flow. The violet
Joins with the star to parable thine eyes,
So meekly bright, so tenderly sublime—

EDITH (*smiling*).

What say the Rocks, and Mountains ?

GERALD.

On the brow
Of the bleak Crag, oft have I marked a flower,
So exquisite in form, in tint so pure,
It seemed the child of dew-drops, and the Sun,
There resting, like a memory of Heaven
In stern, and guilty bosoms. Then, the Vales—
The bright, luxuriant, youngest born of Earth,—
Are they not cradled in the hollow sweep

Of the proud, snow-crowned Titans?   Thus of thee
Tell Rocks, and Mountains, even as gentler things.
My peerless one! whose features are impressed
On all Creation's beauty—I *must* speak,
My heart o'erflows!   Around thee constellate
The symbol glories of the Universe!
I know not if the sense of Beauty change,
When in Eternity, material sight
Dissolves to holier vision; but, methinks,
I should turn coldly from an Angel's glance,
Unless it sembled *thine !*

EDITH.

Cease! cease, my love!
These words bring pain with them.

GERALD.

A novel grief—
To mourn excess in love!

EDITH.

Love me as one
Of Nature's common children—weak enough
To need support, unwary, wanting counsel,—
A weeping, smiling, trusting, doubting girl,
With good intents, marred in the acting oft,
With heaven-ward thoughts that fail through weariness,
And droop the wing, while yet the glance aspires ;—
Having much cause for gratitude,—but more
For penitence,—sincere; yet how infirm !
Oh, let me love! be oftener in thy prayers,
And in thy praises less.

GERALD.

Another sigh !

EDITH.

It came ere I could check it; on my heart
Fear, like the shadow of the Future, fell.
Nay! I have saddened thee.

GERALD.

No more, my Girl,
Of dark forebodings! Lean upon me thus
Thy sweet face just upturned. Now let us thread
This pleasant walk together. I am fain
To drug my Soul with our Futurity,
That it may dream these parting hours away.
Let us o'erlook the transient interval
That severs,—a brief time, but rife with act.
Mine be the struggle! Thou shalt nothing prove
Except the triumph! Mine the throbbing brow,
The midnight labour, and the fevered dream.
Thinkst thou I reck them? No! 'twere proud delight
To shorten temporal life by toil that wins
Enduring good for man! And thou shalt share
The glorious conquest—when the grateful world
Rings with acclaim, I only point to thee—
Thou Genius of my heart! And thus, methinks,
Lips breathing praise, eyes beaming benisons,
We move through ranks of worship,—all our life
A proud procession—

EDITH (apart).

Ending at the tomb.

GERALD (hearing her).

Let the frame rest there! Not with its decay,
The life, and office of true greatness ends;
Its inspiration dwells enshrined in ACT.
A Statue's silence—is the Sculptor's voice.

The Painter's immortality resides
In his own forms, and objects. Attitude,
Expression, light, and shade, the tint so fine
It half eludes the eye,—for Earth retain,
In Death's despite, his *soul!*—And he around
Whose pathway lingered haunting harmonies,
Spirits of Beauty tenanting a sound,—
Lives in his record of their ministry!
Poets, and Sages, thus perpetuate
Their being in the words that age, by age,
Fulfil their lofty ends! Their speech sublime,
Inspires the general heart; their beauty steals
Brightening, and purifying, through the air
Of common life; the Patriot wakes the soul
Of apathetic nations, with their breath
To Freedom's energies; their language gives
Voice to Love's mysteries; the evening hearth
Grows shrine-like, when is hymned their holy chaunt
Of social concord; and their pathos speaks
With a Friend's accent to the desolate!
The thought that *they* were men, makes other men
Exult in manhood; and Eternity
Preaching HEREAFTER to the world, attests
Her Gospel by their deeds! And thus the Sons
Of Genius have prerogative to stand
Exempt from Time's decree; immutable
In change! Though since they were inurned,
States have sprung up,—and died; barbaric lands
Acquired refinement; or realms civilized
Relapsed to old barbarity;—albeit,
Since they trod Earth, the far posterity
Of empires then unknown, in darkness sleep;
Though marvels of their day have dimly waned

To vague tradition ;—Luxury destroyed
The fresh simplicities of primal life,
And added wants to Nature's ;—Science ploughed
Earth's once calm brow in furrows; or proclaimed
New worlds in space ;—still the Perpetual Few
Survive in what they wrought, and sit enthroned,—
Tutelar Spirits of Humanity !

EDITH (*aside*).

Tombs are the Altars of the Great.   Of doom
The intimation haunts me, like the voice
Of distant tides heard faintly from the shores
They overflow hereafter.—(*Aloud.*) Be thy lot
Bright as thy hopes.   God grant it ! but remember
If thou *should'st* fail—that is, if *Men* should fail,—
Mine was a heart that loved thee while the world
Was yet a Stranger. ˙ Prove the world unkind,
That heart is thine still. ˉ

GERALD.

Should the worst befal,
I shall gain strength from this remembrance,
In my soul's weary age to walk erect,
Without the crutch of pity.

EDITH (*reproachfully*).

Gerald !

GERALD.

Speak !

EDITH.

Was that well said ?

GERALD.

I know not ! Should I fail—
Wake to neglect or scorn !—Hence poor distrust !
The omens of my life have been too clear—

Too noble to delude !   No common end
My Past points out.   Believe 'twas not in vain
My young inclinings, spurning common lore,
And saws of village Solons, led my feet
Up mountain heights ere dawn to cheer the Sun
On his great march, and feel that we were born
To kindred destinies ;—or bade me stand
In the deep silence of autumnal woods,
Awed, saddened, solaced, purified, sublimed ;—
Or muse enchanted by the choral streams,
And find my mood to Nature's music set ;—
Or watch at eve the solid orb of fire
Melt in diffusive tenderness, while stole
Into my heart a pensive sanctity,
That made me covet an excuse for tears !

EDITH.

I love to listen !

GERALD.

In my solitude,
While bending o'er the page of Bards, to feel
Their greatness thrill my soul, and albeit then
The lofty meaning I could scarce translate,
To quiver with an awful, vague delight,
And find my heart respond, although the sense
Outran my thought !—What, shall no harvest burst
From seed like this ?   The soil too had its dews,
The softening, kindly influence of love—
Thy love, my bless'd one !   (*A pause, during which
laughter, and voices in conversation, gradually
becoming more distinct, are heard in the lane.*)
Did I hear my name ?

FIRST VOICE.

A kill-joy ! a proud upstart !

SECOND VOICE.

I, myself,
Could turn bell-ringer at his exit.

THIRD VOICE.

Pshaw !
A thumb-snap's notice honours him too much.

EDITH.

Shall we resume our walk ?

GERALD.

Be still as death.

SECOND VOICE.

His very laugh, when he deigned laughter, seemed
To hint good breeding to our noisy mirth ;—
A low, soft laugh—no heart in it.   I hate
A lad that can't laugh !

THIRD VOICE.

Could he clear yon fence?
Or bring his bird down deftly ?

FIRST VOICE.

Ay ! or make
Four runs by one stroke—or with cleaving oar,
Send Lady Violet shooting through the deep
As birds through air ?   Ha ! ha ! (*Loud laughter !*)

SECOND VOICE.

His Father, though,
Rings like true mettle.

THIRD VOICE.

Why the very Sun
We should not miss more than his beaming face,
Telling his white hairs, he is young yet.—Faith !
He's grown as much part of the neighbourhood,
As the old Market Cross; or Roman Arch,
Spanning the highway.

SECOND VOICE.

Do you trust the tales
One hears about that arch?   Is it in nature
Of brick and mortar?

THIRD VOICE.

Is it? I should think so! (*The voices grow confused,
and are shortly lost in the distance.*)

GERALD.

Now will we walk again.

EDITH.

It troubles thee—
This passing folly!

GERALD.

Thy maturer thought
Will prove it Wisdom.   Each Philosophy
Is centred in the being of the Sage—
Or Fool, mayhap—terms are indifferent.
A general error oft is private truth;
What's falsehood here, is there veracity;
The right hand's nothing, is the left hand's all!
For natures as they limit, or expand,
Determine faith or doubt,—ourselves the bound
To our own fate.   That Caterpillar's bliss
Is in luxuriant idleness to crawl
O'er the sweet leaves of roses, wondering
Why yonder Bee should wear his wings with toil,
Touring from flower to flower. Perchance the Bee
Much marvels that the Ringdove builds her nest
So high, that garden odours, and the scent
Of thyme-banks reach it not.   That very Dove
Hath never solved the charm the Martlet finds
In eaves of human dwellings ; unto *him*
'Tis mystery why the kingly Eagle dwells

On the rock's peak in solitude.   We judge
Out of our life—or want of it;—our friends
Who passed just now, from theirs—*which was not mine.*
Since men must measure; let them—and in dreams,
Belt great Orion, with a wisp of hay!

EDITH.

Bethink thee, love! they are thy fellow men.

GERALD.

Doubtless!   We all need raiment, food, and graves.
If that make not relationship—what can ?

EDITH.

Ah, love!   I would not have these moods recur
In which thou spurnest so the humbler minds.
Perchance there is less difference in men,
Than the great deem.   The coarse, unlettered hind,
May not discern the truth in thy high words,
Nor in thy fine, and airy thoughts, perceive
The feelings they unfold.   Yet trust me, love!
Feelings are like in most men, though the forms
Which they put on be diverse.   Sympathies
Most deep, and holy, often stir in hearts,
That have few words to shape them; even as streams
Embosomed in the earth, refresh its plains;
While the broad river, open to the sun,
And mirror of his light, can do no more!

GERALD.

'Tis sweetly reasoned, Edith.

EDITH.

Oh say—*truly.*

GERALD.

Truly—if power be evidence of truth;
Strange, how brief simple syllables from thee

Charm from my breast its bitterness.   With love
My spirit thrills to all things.   I could sue
For an affront—to pardon it !   Henceforth
Thou shalt atone all men to me—

EDITH.

Beware !
Oh ! I should chide ; but that we part so soon.

GERALD.

Chide on—the tones will contradict the words—
But hark ! the wicket sighs upon its hinge.

EDITH.

See, 'tis thy Father !—Gerald, one request !
Thou and thy Sire, though linked by natural bonds,
The dearest Nature owns,—are yet distinct,—
I may say opposite, in taste, in plans,
Objects, and studies.   He a homely man
Whose interests live in themes of every day ;
His comrades, simple, unambitious folk
Who watch the seasons with an anxious eye,
Solicitous for Summer's genial showers,
And cloudless skies in Autumn ;—their discourse
Pleasant, and kindly,—still by limits bound
Too narrow for thy scope.   Now much I fear
Thy father mourns this difference, deeming scorn
Prompts thy disrelish of his humble joy,
Wherein 'tis clear he errs.   'Twas Nature's will—
Not thine,—which this diversity begat.
To blame thee were unjust !   Still for my sake,
On this our parting eve indulge his vein ;
Conform thy mood to his.   One sympathy
Ye have in common,—that of generous hearts !
He tarries at the gate.—Come !

GERALD.

May Heaven bless thee,
Sweet Minister of concord.   (*They walk towards the
       gate.*)

EDITH (*to* EUSTACE).

Welcome home.

EUSTACE (*turning*).

Ha ! Woodpecker.

EDITH.

Where lay your evening walk ?   (*The church clock
       strikes.*)
What, eight already !   You are late to-night,
I'll scarce forgive you—though I own the charm
These cooler hours possess to tempt the feet ;—
The fragrant scent of meadows, and the sheen
Of daisies, and the golden buttercups ;
The shadowed lane whose quiet deeper grows
From lulling melodies of happy birds ;
The balm, and beauty of the clustering rose—
That dear wild-rose, which so profusely hangs
As Flora on her gala day had cast
A wreath to every bush !

EUSTACE.

There *Gerald* spoke—
These phrases are too fine for such as I.

GERALD (*to* EDITH).

Where least like me, you please my Father best.

EUSTACE.

I said not that, exactly.

EDITH.

No ! nor meant it.

EUSTACE.

Not I ! In that huge, noisy, smoky town,
To which he hastens, he'll not find a friend
To beat his Father.

GERALD (*grasping his hand*).

There—nor in the world.

EUSTACE.

Whist ! That's enough, my lad—(*a Stage Coach turns
the corner of the road*)—
And in good time,
Here comes the Highflyer. Jenkins, good night.
A first-rate whip is Jenkins, and his team
Were credit to the mail : well blown, old Andrew !
I never sleep well having missed that horn.

GERALD.

Granted fine weather, and an honest heart,
Few stations match the outside of a Stage.

EUSTACE.

Ah ! say you so ?

GERALD.

Soon as you climb the roof
Anticipation glows. In heightened ear,
And pawing hoof of each impatient steed,
Already you partake the inspiring whirl,
The freshening gale, the glad variety
Of ever shifting landscape ! With his arm
Pillowed on one sleek courser's back, the groom,
Rightfully proud, the parting signal waits ;
While notes the urchin group, with wistful glance,
The busy preparation, or the sun
Dance on the sparkling loops of polished brass.
At length ascends the portly charioteer.

One hurried hum of farewell; one " God speed;"
And off you rattle o'er the cheering stones,
By lively houses to whose thresholds rush
The greeting inmates at the wonted sound;
While the brave bugle peals a blithe good-bye,
And promise of return to all the Town !

EUSTACE.

Bravo!   Go on.

GERALD.

Familiar suburbs next
Glide by, till through the toll-bar's friendly gate
Unchecked you shoot.   Now comes the open road,
Bordered with blooming hedgerows, which divide
From pleasant pastures, where the startled sheep
Gaze upward as you pass; anon you sweep
Through merry hamlets where the cottage porch
Rich roses, and the pendant woodbine screen;
While from the gardens some protruding branch
Admonishes the traveller's head to bend.
There in the distance stately turrets rise;
There in the depths, an architectural dream,
Some fair retreat lies bosomed.   Now the hills
In quick succession tower; yet not retard
The eager steeds, borne by the impetus
Of one descent unto the following height,
Ere yet they seem to climb!   You pause awhile
On the proud eminence, and at a glance
A tract of miles survey; the rippling corn,
The silver threads of intersecting streams,
The graceful spires, witness of villages
The eye detects not—but again you dive
In arborescent vales!

EUSTACE.

Well said! well said!
I am not tired at all; tell us the rest
While we walk round the garden.

GERALD.

Nay, 'tis done.
We're almost at the journey's end, I fear—
But what of that? Delicious in the dusk
Of days so spent, is the concluding stage
Our trusty coach fulfils, when passengers
Remark what signs foretell approaching home,
Dwell on expectant kindred lingering
By the inn door, and deeming every sound
The hum of distant wheels. And when arrived,
How sweet the welcome Brethren interchange;
Or Child with Parent!—See the Sire at length
To his own hearth restored! What thankful peace
Shines in his Consort's smile! The very room
Wears a surpassing look of happiness.
The urn so brightly gleams, the coffee yields
Such rich aroma—all things are improved—
Save Time, who gallops faster than his wont,
While wondrous stories of far cities charm
The ear of wife and children; and their eyes
Beam at the tokens of remembering love,
A shawl or dress; a picture-book—or toy!

EDITH.

Thanks, dearest! (*To* EUSTACE). He deserves a recompense
For that sweet sketch.

GERALD.

The Artist is o'erpaid
By thine approval—and his Father's.

EUSTACE.

Now—
Can't you forego this London scheme, my lad ?
Well, well; I will not ask it; you look grave,
Go,—and God bless you !

GERALD.

I shall come again.
Meanwhile my thoughts will oft revisit home,
And in the crowded street, or solitude,
Shall fancy shape it to my glistening eye.

EUSTACE (*walking on*).

Well, let us in.

GERALD (*delaying, to* EDITH).

How is it with thee, love ?

EDITH.

'Tis happy sadness, dearer than content !

GERALD.

Kin to the solemn beauty of the hour.
The twilight shades steal on, the silver mists
Descend on hill, and tree, and sacred fane.
And Nature's face a calm, pure look assumes,
As though about to sleep, her day's task done,
She knew her head was pillowed at God's feet,
And that His eye was on her.   Beautiful !

EUSTACE.

Gerald, my boy, where art thou ?

GERALD (*bounding forward with* EDITH).

At thy side !

REVERIE.

REVERIE.

SCENE.—*London. A pleasant apartment in which* GERALD *is discovered writing.**

GERALD (*laying aside his pen*).

Rejoice my soul! Thy travail now is o'er,
To thee an offspring born, whose sight repays
The glorious agony her mother bore!
How doth this hour atone for anxious days,
And nights of vigil! Lo the living mind
Sees in this fragile page, herself enshrined;
Her feelings, musings, " faculties divine,"
Breathe in the words, and animate the line!

My book! my poem. Daughter of my Soul!
What are thy destinies? Let Fancy's eye
Trace thy career until it reach the goal
Of Fame perpetual. Thy bright ministry
My spirit yearns to shape.—

Within her hall,
Where through kind screens the softened sunbeams fall,

---

* The Author is desirous of claiming for the following lines the full distinction between the soliloquy and the reverie. They are intended to represent thoughts which one would scarcely express in language to oneself—far less to another—involuntary thoughts by which the mind is borne along without any conscious effort of its own.

And on some terrace near, is heard at play
The veiled voice of the fountains, doth recline,
In witching negligence, a noble maid.
Her eyes are bent upon the Poet's lay,
And as she reads with holy light they shine ;
Partaker of his Being is she made !
Around her all that luxury supplies
To charm the sense attends, and to her ear
Are nightly breathed Devotion's dulcet sighs ;
Her queenly brow hath lineal right to wear
The circlet by Baronial Normans worn :
Yet, as she reads, her mind is upward borne
By the Companion Spirit ; and she owns
A loftier pride than earthly state imparts ;
While dwarfs the wide inheritance of thrones,
To that which Genius founds in human hearts.
From all that only *seems* her soul is free,
And learns a season, what it is—*to be !*

I follow thee again, my child, my song !—
Some glorious autumn eve, 'neath green arcades
Dimming the natural aisles with holy shades,
Wrapt in communion tender, wend along
Two forms : how stately his,—while meeker grace
Dwells in her movements, timorous with joy.
Little they speak. The heart upon the face
Writes meanings, which in words they fain would trace ;
But all their language doth the truth alloy,
More than impart. " See—that delicious nook,"
She saith ; " There will we rest, and from the book,
Thy gift this morning, shalt thou read awhile."
" Of love ?" he answers, and assents her smile.
He reads. Oh, marvel ! Not a throb, a thought,

A dream, a yearning which themselves have known—
But into kindling speech the Bard hath wrought,
And all *their* life recorded in *his own*—
The pangs that pleased them more than common mirth,
The pride of sacrifice, the bliss of tears,
The myriad fancies that in one have birth,
The Epoch hours to which the coming years
Pay tribute for delicious memories—
Are all emblazoned on his wondrous scroll,
Whose Being doth the World epitomize,
Whose Art the Soul interprets—to the Soul!

Who is't that musing paces through his room
Ere tender twilight deepens into gloom?
The silver lamp unlighted, from the fire
Red gleams by turns advance, by turns retire;
Yet of that fitful light at times the glow
Illumes the form, or glances on the brow,
Or with a steadier flame defines the air
Of him who moves in meditation there.

The Minister whose Titan Spirit guides
A Nation's progress, and whose will decides
The fate of generations—it is he
Who wanders in the shadow musingly.
Where tend his thoughts?   Recals he now the wrong
Wrought by the narrow soul, and venomed tongue?
Invokes he energy to meet the blow
He marks impending from a worthier foe?
Or doth the weight of care his mind oppress—
The loftiest sometimes faint—with weariness?
Ah, no! from him this hour are distant far
The aims, and harass of the public war.

c

The Minstrel's page with idle hand turned o'er
Hath won upon his heart, and waked once more
The blest familiars of his youth to life—
The generous thoughts with love and beauty rife.
The noise of crowds, the hum of distant wheels
That with them bear the restless, or the gay,
Break on his loneliness; but o'er *him* steals
The tranquil memory of a brighter day,
And lovelier scene.   His home amid the trees
Salutes his eye, and on his brow the breeze
That fanned his youthful temples, seems to play;
Throng round Companions of an earlier state—
The blithe, the full of hope, the fond, the free,
Who once predicting that he might be great,
Still claimed an interest in his memory!
And one upon whose ear his accents fell
In first devotion's trembling, tender tone—
She who first felt how potent was the spell
Of eloquence, a World had yet to own.
Oh, happy hours, when if he sighed for fame,
'Twas more her fortune, than his own to bless,
That he might wreath around *her future name*
        The laurel of success!

Thus hast thou wrought in him, my child, my song!
A gentler influence, a nobler will;
His heart thy gracious echoes doth prolong:
He seeks the Senate; but they haunt him still,
And in that purer hour he yields a grace
How often sought, but never hoped before,
While deaf to common plaudits, steals the face
Before his vision, of the blessing poor!
Whence did the State its inspiration draw
Of mercy?   'Twas the Poet framed the law.

Another revelation !   All alone,
As silence mute, and motionless as stone,
Attired in sable robes that yet appear
Bright to the mourning which her features wear—
The childless Mother of the Orphan stands ;
Her eye undimmed by tears, unwrung her hands,—
Stands at her casement, while the world rolls by
Like a strange void in which she hath no part,
Its changing aspects nothing to her eye,
Its myriad interests nothing to her heart.
Repinings ne'er escape her.   Why complain ?
The wailing voice brings not the lost again.
And in that wordless agony, her day
And night like shadows come and flit away.
In all the outward life she duly lives,
To all who speak the answer meet she gives ;
Rises, and dons her garments when the light
Tells at her lattice of the parted night,
Partakes of viands on her table spread,
Walks in the paths she used of yore to tread,
And if saluted as she lonely wends,
In answering courtesy her body bends ;
And when the day is spent, her taper's beam
Conducts her to her chamber—not to dream,
But still on each returning night, is press'd
Her couch in silence—others deem it rest.
Times are, when few from the external guess
The spirit's rapture, or its wretchedness ;
" The heart," 'tis writ, " knows its own bitter lot,
And with its joy, a stranger meddleth not !"

Strange, how, in desolation, Love will cling
To every object that the past can bring,

Though but in thought, again!   Thus did she look,
That lonely mourner, on an after eve,
O'er many a faded letter, many a book,
O'er many a trinket, and one auburn tress,
Many a little cap, and folded dress
That long had lacked a wearer.   I believe,
That as the Mother turned her relics o'er,
Her heart was nigh to breaking; still she bore
The pang in silence.   But what meets her eye?
A slender volume, on whose opening leaf
Are words inscribed, so tender, though so brief,
That all the pathos of the soul seems shed
In that short sentence—written by the dead!
Her Husband's gift while yet in doubt he wooed,
And through its maze of wiles her love pursued—
From that sad page her glance she would refrain,
And shun its fascination; but in vain.
Strange sorceries in the lines her gaze control,
And through the subject sense arrest the soul!

She reads; the strain is sorrowful, and tells
How marriage peals were changed to funeral knells;
How Death stood darkly in the shadowed porch,
When swept the bridal party from the church;
And smiled to think how soon the gladsome train,
With heavier tread, should trace that path again.

Seven suns were numbered from her nuptial morn,
When to her grave the ill-starred bride was borne.
In her cold hand the rose, scarce withered, lay,
That graced her bosom on her marriage day;
And of the flowers wherewith the maids had strowed,
In farewell love, their favourite's bridal road,

The leaves, the moralising wind had swept
O'er the green coverlet 'neath which she slept!

The verse records how on that fearful night,
The Bridegroom took his solitary flight,
And roamed beneath the stars for many a league,
With strength that, born of madness, mocked fatigue.
How to his mind, through many vacant days,
His loss loomed dimly through the shadowy haze
Of thought distempered; till the uncertain dream
Melted before the mind's returning beam,
Which, as the wreathing mists their veils up-furled,
Disclosed a barren and unpeopled world!

And as the mourner reads, a softening spell
Steals o'er her soul! " *The Bard whose tender line*
Hath told this Bridegroom's grief so passing well,
Perchance might penetrate, and pity mine!"

But now the strain reveals the gentler mood
Wrought in his breast by Time;—Despair subdued
To pensiveness which from the Future drew
A present hope, as one may see the yew
Shrine in its heart of shade, the brightness caught
From the horizon's lustre—how he wrought
Good deeds as tributes to *her* memory,
And cherished most the faith that to *her* eye
His heart and acts were open; till a sense
Of union with celestial Influence,
Of spiritual ties, his mind possessed,
And if delusive, while beguiling, blest;
Shed through his spirit a benign repose,
A love that ministered to others' woes,

And thus assuaged his own; a genial power
To gather meanings from a cloud, or flower,
Contentment in the present, and the faith
To which unfold the ebon gates of Death;
While the fair vista of the Land of Light
Already opens on the purer sight!

That lonely mourner reads.   Ah, no; her eyes
Are dimmed by the returning sympathies!
Descend upon her sterile soul the dews
Which quicken, or revive, as they diffuse.
She feels at length; she weeps, she hopes, she prays;
Her prayer is humble, and its issue—praise.
And like the viewless odours which exhale,
When rains have ceased, upon the freshened gale,
Reviving Immortalities dispense,
Through all her soul, a blissful influence,
And in her spirit, hopeful and serene,
Awakes "the Evidence of Things Unseen."
Ah sure the sacred pathway to the skies
Winds through the region of the sympathies;
The Realm of Feeling to the Bard is given,
A Human Empire, but it neighbours Heaven!

Child of my Soul, go forth—from every mind
To draw emotions fresh, or thought refined!
Visit the poor; sweeten their daily toil
Who ply the loom, or cultivate the soil,
And by a holier world's expectant bliss,
Lighten the load, and soothe the pains of this.
What though the plan of Providence decree
In Time, strange contrast, wide disparity;

Though wealth, and want—servility, and pride—
Infirmity, and might—tread side by side,
And 'neath what Misery deems th' unequal skies,
The Lordly Hall, and penal Poorhouse rise !
How sweet the thought—from fortunes bright or stern,
Alike may *pious souls* a meetness learn
For their awaiting home—the rich, and great,
To guard and succour men of lowly state,
And half anticipating Heaven's employ,
To Earth be Angels, Ministers of joy—
The poor by sacred trust, endurance still,
And meek submission to the Eternal Will,
To prove how Faith that brings the Future near,
The Present too, can sanctify, and cheer !

Beyond the grave ! All difference ceases there
Save that of Nature; and the trappings rare
Of wealth, and rule—of lineage, and clan—
No more adorn, or hide—*the virtual man !*
There, stripped of all conventional disguise,
To Judgment's ken the *spirit* open lies,
In its own being, dark or bright, to find
Its fate recorded, and its rank assigned.
Heaven's glance reads inly ! 'tis a common truth,
The world hath conned it from Creation's youth;
Ah ! what a change would Wisdom's lore impart,
Were all we learn by *rote*, acquired by *heart !*

Go forth my Song—To age's Winter bring
Again, the radiance of life's genial Spring.
Amidst the desert parched of busy years,
Once more unseal the precious fount of tears.

In Mammon's empire still assert thy claim
To prompt the impulse warm, and lofty aim;
And in the rural hamlets, where the maids
Yet turn the humming wheel, 'neath beech-wood shades,
Charm with the simple beauty of thy lay
Hymned by their lips—those tranquil hours away!—

Oh, joy!—To perfect, though through doubt, and care,
Some common blessing in which all may share.
Oh, happy labour, that in love can bind
Thus to our hearts in every grade—our kind!
Oh, dear delight, whene'er the crowded street
We thread, or rove through sylvan haunts—to greet
With silent welcome every form we see,
And inly murmur—"*I have toiled for thee!*"

Ah! Lady of my Love—that thou wert nigh
To share these feelings, that I might behold
My vague, wild rapture, mirrored in thine eye,
And grow assured in bliss; while instinct fine,
Transcending speech, should to thy heart unfold
The subtlest, tenderest mysteries, of mine.

(*He goes to the window.*)

Now will I wend abroad—the moonbeams quiver
Already on the wide and dusky river,
And in a softened, dreamlike stillness, stand
The long continuous piles that gird the strand.
Day's busy march is o'er, and from the street
The calmer echoes come of leisure feet.
The turmoil of existence fainter grows,
And e'en the populous city owns repose.

Forth will I to the Minster bridge to-night,
And watch—*around*, the shadowy domes and spires;
Below, some sail flit through the silver light;
Above, the sacred and unfailing fires;
While in my heart, as in the scene, combine
Harmoniously, the human—and divine!

THE WORLD.

PART I.

[An interval of two years is supposed to have elapsed
between this and the preceding part.]

THE WORLD.

SCENE.—*A Boudoir in a stately Mansion, overlooking an extensive Park.*

LORD *and* LADY ROXMORE.

LORD ROXMORE.

The Sun is high in Heaven, and o'er the slopes
The trees scant shadows cast; the fleecy cloud,
Scarce more substantial than the gossamer,
No zephyr bears through space, nor ripple breaks
The lakelet's sheeted silver.   See! the deer
In happy lassitude, beneath the elms,
Find shelter and repose.   This dreamy time
Hath a beguiling and peculiar charm;
Here screened from heat by plants thine art hath trained
To creep around our casement, hour by hour
I were content to linger—nought to list
Except thy voice, and but thy smile to watch!

LADY ROXMORE.

Ah, Courtier!

LORD ROXMORE.

Fairest sceptic—dost thou doubt?

LADY ROXMORE.

I fear that *you* would weary.   For myself,
'Tis certainty.

LORD ROXMORE.

Can Love grow weary then?

LADY ROXMORE.

" Can Love grow weary then?"—so plaintively!
Make thine own heart the oracle of mine.

Can Love grow weary?   No! but Fancy may,
And passion must—as here the Bard asserts,
In apter phrase than mine.—(*Reads*)—

" *They love indeed*
Whose hearts religion hallows, and whose deeds
A heavenly law subserve.   The Passion roused
By mere material blandishments—the flush
That mantles in an Houri's face, the fires
Seductive of her eye, the glowing frame
Ripening to Beauty's fulness—are of Earth,
And wake but earthly impulse, fiercely brief!
The countless ambushed arts, and subtle wiles
Of Woman's captivation—loveliness
By wit enlivened, and bright satire's shaft,
For the fair archer's grace at once forgiven;
The natural artifice of attitude,
Descending tresses whose soft shadows play
Like darkening dimples—on an ivory neck.
The head declining on the snowy arm
Conscious of gradual curve, and polished round,
The mignon foot escaping from the folds
Of the free careless robe—but Fancy fire,
With whom caprice is nature.   Love alone—
The attraction, magnetism, sympathy,
That Virtue bears to Virtue, is eterne!
The pure is the immortal—Holiness
Thy fount, Eternity!   Thus love to God
And all his attributes, must still precede
Enduring human love.   And then how bless'd
The intercourse, the unity of hearts!
Their common sense of beauty, mutual aims
For all that raises Earth, or draws down Heaven;
The growing meetness for an after sphere,

And yet withal, a deepening joy in this—
Joy in the prospect, in the actual joy—
In aspiration lofty, hope sublime,
And sympathies whose only voice is tears—
Mortality's concession to the soul
Whose extacy is tongueless!   Still, with these,
What calm delight in all the homely forms
And offices of Life !   The eye that reads
The planets, finds dear beauty in the flower;
The ear that anthems ravish, is attuned
To voice of pipe, and timbrel; and the heart—
Sweet mediator between mind, and sense—
Makes the august familiar, and exalts
The common to the great."

LORD ROXMORE.

Oh ! be our love
Of this complexion ; we are newly wed,
And all is brightness yet.   May never cloud
Our clear horizon dim.

LADY ROXMORE.

Desire not that !
This life is progress ; for the *better* still :
We hope and strive ; and oft adversity
Is Truth's best teacher—stimulates to life
Else dormant qualities, invokes our faith,
Submission, and endurance.   Hear again
How deals the Poet with this very theme.—(*Reads*)—

" Oh ! in our days of early love, when o'er thy form and
　　　face,
There breathed an atmosphere of joy, and ever changing
　　　grace ;

With sparkling eye, and braidless tress, and smooth
　　　　unshadowed brow,
Of every maid beneath the Heavens, the brightest,
　　　　blithest—*thou !*

I prayed that not a tint of grief, or casual cloud of woe
Might o'er thy sunny stream of life one darkening image
　　　　throw ;
And that unvexed by storm, thy Time, with half uncon-
　　　　scious motion,
Might lapse into Eternity—as rivers into ocean.

But when thine hour of sorrow came, and every wounded
　　　　feeling
Fled to my sympathetic love, for comfort and for healing,
Till sighs were hushed in thankfulness, and of the hand
　　　　I press'd
The tremulous quivering testified how suffering might
　　　　be bless'd.

Bless'd—in the hidden mines of love, it opens to the day,
Bless'd—in the inner springs it moves, externally to play ;
Bless'd—in the privilege it yields of *trusting*, in our grief,
Bless'd—in the tenderness whose balm is dearer than relief!

Then praised I Him who fashioned thus these mystic
　　　　hearts of ours,
Not merely for glad faculties, and all the smiling powers!
But for capacities of grief, and visitings of care,
Wherein Love claims prerogative to solace—or to share!"

LORD ROXMORE.

Most true—my heart responds to every line ;

And I confess a debt of gratitude
To this same Gerald Lovel.   Is the name
Much bruited in the world?

LADY ROXMORE.

I know not that,
Nor him—except that better part of Man,
The spirit here embodied.   Pleasant, though,
This chance encounter with a noble mind,
Like to some image of a Saint, that meets
The Pilgrim's eye abroad, and on his way
With sacred thoughts awakened, sends him forth!

———

Scene.—*A Room in* Ashton's *House at Bayswater.*

GERALD *and* Ashton.

ASHTON.

'Tis sheer hallucination!

GERALD.

As you will.
The slighting name cannot unmake a truth;
Nor sounding diction render falsehood real.

ASHTON.

But to the point.   *Are* moods of fancy real?

GERALD.

Most real, most actual—

ASHTON.

Dreams!

GERALD.

Which dreams are real—
Even as those which to the Elder Seers
Divine monitions, heavenly guidance—brought.
In Dreams the Past relives, and o'er the scene

Where ages gone, heroic deeds were done;
Where lovers roved whose faithfulness is writ
In Minstrels' chronicles; where mused the wise
Whose currency of thought, than gold more rich,
Bought truth for generations—still preside
The Warrior, Lover, Sage—to consecrate
The soil they trod.   To Fancy's vision rapt,
Nature reveals her mission.   Not a hue
That wakes an Isle of Beauty in the air,
Nor breeze, nor zephyr, nor the branch that waves
Obedient to their impulse, but fulfils
A gracious ministry—renews the mind
For all its earthly travail, or consoles
With whispers of Hereafter.   What! deny
Imagination actual that doth blend
The Past and Future in our span of years—
Making us Lords of Ages, strengthening faith
In that inheritance where Time entranced
By the unuttered loveliness, forgets
His pinions' use for ever?   Deem'st it nought
Imagination's Ararat to climb?
While they who scorn it round the narrow shred
Of temporal existence, faintly grope,
Circled by ceaseless twilight, and the wave
That day by day, encroaches on their strip—
To overwhelm it soon!

ASHTON.

Bravely thrown out!
Just emphasis, appropriate action, life!
Nonsense delivered *con amore!*   Eh?
                    (*After a pause.*)
Though scarce a veteran, Lovel! still my years
By ten outnumber thine.   Of men, and things,

More knowledge have I gained, and to account—
I speak not vainly—have my notings turned.
Be counselled now. 'Tis wiser policy
Mankind to *please*—than *teach*. And in my view.
There seems scant need for teaching. In the realms
Of Thought, and Nature; in Theology,
Philosophy, the Arts and Sciences—
E'en in Mechanic crafts—all seems complete.
What have we yet to learn?

GERALD.

In sacred forms,
Too oft the *spirit;* in Philosophy,
The *wisdom of the heart !* in Science, this—
That to dissect a flower, to decompose
A fluid to its gases, or invent
Biographies for fossils—fills not quite
The range of human faculty—nay, leaves
Rare secrets yet unfolded. Ay! perchance
A sweeter lore dwells in the dewy leaf
Of some Eve-nurtured rose, or violet—
Than in the thesis fine that pertly struts
With sonorous nomenclature in its train—
Calyx and stamen; pistil and corolla!

ASHTON.

You phantom-chasers ever thus contemn
The real and useful. I can comprehend
The claims of Physics, and esteem him wise
Whose toil hath made him master of their laws,
And operation. But your *abstract* flights
And *undemonstrated* Ideals, work
Mere present fantasy, and late regret.
Give me the senses for my guides in life;
I'll trust none other.

GERALD.

Come, then, solve me this,
But—by the aid of sense.   Which higher ranks—
The Exchange—or Temple?   On that point consult
The Architect—or better say—the Mason,
Who knows the several cost of rearing both.
Where differs Marathon from common earth?
Why claims precedence vaunting Runnymede?
Doth there the husbandman find richer soil,
Crops more luxuriant, than in nameless plains?
Pshaw! bound belief by sight—our homes are nought
Save brick and mortar, and our Fathers' graves
But ordinary stone;—Eternity
A solemn juggle, and high Heaven—a dream!

ASHTON.

Stay! there's a wholesome medium.

GERALD.

No! the right
Lies ever in extremes.   Of all the saws
That ever duped the world, that " *mediate*" saw
Hath wrought most bane to man.   If truth be truth,
It may not be compounded without sin!

ASHTON.

Well, Gerald!—I am loath enough to press
This argument against thee—but observe,
Mine, is the verdict of the multitude.
'Tis an old adage that what all *affirm*
Hath reason in't; and so what all *deny*—
Or at the least neglect—*must* prove unsound.
Now in this very strait, my friend, art thou—
A Sage without disciples, Labourer
Without toil's meet reward, and though possessed

Of talents which might stead thee, win thee fame
And wealth, the which thou need'st—forgive me—poor!

GERALD.

Well.

ASHTON.

Well! Will Imagination feed, and clothe,—
Defend from cold, or shade from heat? *It may.*
You who live *out of Sense,* perhaps have quelled
The *needs* of Sense!

GERALD.

The jest is excellent!

ASHTON.

Nay, now! Be rational—Of natural gifts
My portion doth not far thine own exceed—
Yet look ye, how *I* prosper.

GERALD.

Very true.

ASHTON.

Think you 'twas the Ideal lined my floor
With this soft carpet, or that couch disposed
In tempting negligence, or graced my walls
With such adornings as you see? No! no,
I owe these to two agents much despised,
But very powerful—One is Industry;
The other—Good, Sound Sense!

GERALD (*involuntarily*).

This world's children
Are in their generation—

ASHTON.

What?

GERALD.

I say
Good sense works wonders.

ASHTON.

Wilt be serious?
A wise man, let me tell you, pushes on
Straight to the golden goal.　To him each path
Of human travel—be it politics,
Or war, or trade, or letters—*ends the same.*
An Author's needs not be a thriftless lot;
Only keep open eyes.—Nicely observe
What suits the hour, what themes are in men's mouths,
What interests TO-DAY.　A great man dies—
Then 'tis *your* legacy, to write his life.
A dissolution threatens—out at once
With a smart, caustic pamphlet.　It may chance
A noted person—much in the world's mind—
Trips in his course, mistakes his cue, or yields
On sudden to temptation—Quiz him straight—
Provoke the laugh, and point the jibe.　Enough!
I might go on till sunset, but you catch
The pith of the thing already.

GERALD.

Bear with me.
Through life, I have been servant to my moods,
And could but act by their inclining.　These
Have ever drawn me from the noisy world
Of petty interest, unworthy strife,
Low ends, and lower means, and bound my fate
With Hopes that scale the dark material walls
Obscuring heaven from man; with Sympathies
That I ne'er found embodied—*saving once;*
And with " *Hallucinations* " that were *Facts*
To me, and *one* beside.　And these unseen
But actual consorts of a life, else lone,
Were, as I deemed, for highest use vouchsafed.

I may be wrong in *that*, and I confess
The lot my fancy pictured, daily dims
In my horizon.   All my purposes
Heaven may withstand, and cast my life away
As an unseasonable weed—Well! well,
I cannot alter now, nor bend my mind
To common uses.   I would rather die,—
Death consecrates, but change degrades,—yes, die!

ASHTON.

I gather from this moving speech, you chafe
Because the world prefers plain prose to rhyme,
Reality to fancy, and dull fact
To poet's fiction.

GERALD.

Fiction !   Poetry
Lives but by truth.   Truth is its heart.   Bards write
The life of soul—the *only* life.   Each line
Breathes life—or *nothing*.   Fiction ! Who narrates
The stature of a man, his gait, his dress,
The colour of his hair, what meats he loved,
Where he abode, what haunts he frequented,
His place and time of birth, his age at death,
And how much crape and cambric mourned his end—
Writes a *biography!*   But who records
The yearnings of the heart, its joys, and pangs,
Its alternating apathy, and hope,
Its stores of memory which the richer grow
The longer they are hived, its faith that stands
Upon the grave, and counts it as a beach
Whence souls embark for home, its prayers for man,
Its trust in Heaven, despite of man—writes *fiction !*
Get a new lexicon.

ASHTON.

Most exemplary Bard!
Your Poets, then, have never gilded vice
With beauty's specious surface; never lent
A charm to sensuous passion; never woke
A blush on Virtue's cheek; never sworn troth
To Bacchus, or the fair frail Paphian!

GERALD.

Never *as* Poets. The Man bred the sin,
And stole the Poet's garb to hide its shame—
The form was hideous; the garb—beauty, still!

ASHTON.

Well! I could almost love thee for this folly,
And my heart yearns to thee, as doth it not
To many a wiser man. But tell me, Gerald,
How may I aid thee? Thou art passing poor,
And Song has nought with lucre. Listen, now:
I have a worthy friend—a thriving merchant,
A keen, sharp-sighted veteran, who carved
With his own hands, his road to Fortune's heights;
And yet withal an honest, liberal soul,
And one who loves his fellows. I will plead
Your cause with him, for you have faculties,
Learning, ay, and quick sense, too, when you list—
Might serve in his vocation.

GERALD (*musingly*).

'Tis well meant.

ASHTON.

Thou art offended!

GERALD.

No! That grasp is friendship's
And gratitude's. I frankly tell you, Ashton,

My follies, as you deem them, have absorbed
The whole of my small store.   I could not bear
To draw from my good Father's charities
Aught more than my just portion—*that* is gone!
One lives, whose slender fortunes all were mine,
Did I but *hint* of need.   But half my dream
Was to achieve her greatness.   I would starve,
Ere be her pensioner!   I *do* accept
Most frankly, then, your aid, and here devote
My head and hands to any honest toil,
With the poor privilege of leisure dreams—
If I *can* dream again.

ASHTON.

That's rightly said.
Come!   Shall we court the air, and see what face
The world wears out of doors—stroll through the park,
Or loiter by the ring—my frequent haunt?
There shall you note some tasteless millionaire
Lost in his ponderous, and blazing cage—
Long Acre's rolling satire—thunder by;
While my Lord's apter fancy—noiseless, light,
And toned with grateful coolness to the view—
Glides in the rear.   And there in listless grace—
Her easy car seems more to sail, than roll—
Float's Fashion's Cynosure, her governed mien
To none revealing that she marks or heeds
The ardent homage of the straining eye,
Or licensed insult of the fixed lorgnette.
What! Art thou dreaming?   Brood not thus alone,—
'Tis sorriest vanity that makes us think
Our thoughts our best companions.   Seek the throng,
Join in the dance, bend o'er the Siren's chair,

D

Rebut with grace the point of Beauty's wit,
Your features turn to words ; your smiles to thoughts.
     (*Drawing on his gloves.*)
Be more alive—You are too modest, man !
Too self-depreciating, too inconfident,
To sparkle in *réunions.*

GERALD.

Do you think so ?   [*They go out.*

THE WORLD.

PART II.

THE WORLD.

SCENE.—*Garden in front of* EUSTACE LOVEL's *Cottage.*

EDITH *and* MARGARET.

MARGARET.

Ah, young lady ! 'tis a heavy stroke, and hard to bear.
To think now that he has been our Landlord these
fifteen years, and was never before asked a day's grace
in the matter of rent!

EDITH.

But he is not deaf, surely, to the plea of misfortunes
so numerous, so sudden ! Either he has not heard of
these calamities, or he has misconceived their history.

MARGARET.

Not he ! Not he ! 'Twas in his own grounds my
George was made a cripple by the chance blow of his
scythe. None knows better than the Squire, that the lad,
by that mishap, lost two months' work; and that all his
spare earnings went in Doctors' drugs. He knows, too,
how the cold Spring winds stripped the trees of half their
blossoms, and how the blight devoured what the wind
spared.—Ah ! 'tis not the opportunity to know, that he
wants, but the heart to feel. But for your sweet self,
Miss Edith, and Master Lovel, we had starved outright
ere this.

EDITH.

I trust not, Margaret ! I have heard of many in

yonder town, who delight to relieve the necessities of the
deserving.

MARGARET.

Ay! ay, lady-bird. Had I been comely, or newly-
widowed—or had my George been a flaxen-headed,
blue-eyed boy of four—many's the dame had rested
by my door-way, begged my new milk, and paid me
with a crown-piece! But you see there was nothing
to take—to *interest;* that's the word—in our case: I
am not particular well-favoured, and my Son's grown
up—beside which, he's a spice of pride in his natur,
and will bear a load above his strength without asking
other people's help. Oh! 'tis your quiet, drudging,
plain-going misery, that's least cared for. Tears that
roll at leisure down pale delicate faces, every hand
wipes off—but as for tears that ooze down cheeks
toil-worn, and sun-tanned—why, the sun may dry
them.

EDITH.

You speak too bitterly.

MARGARET.

Ah, Lady! you have no trouble.

EDITH (*smiling sadly*).

You are wrong. I have my share.

MARGARET.

What! Have you ever turned to the chimney nook
in which you have sat night by night, summer and
winter, for fifteen years; have you seen there the one
elbow chair with the bit of cushion at its back, where
once rested the dear head that has now the ground for
its pillow? Have you done this, and felt what 'twould
be to quit for ever your dear old home, without a roof,
save Heaven, to shelter you?

EDITH.

And with Him who dwells there, to direct your way.
Forget not that—

MARGARET (*disregarding her*).

In straits like this, you have not heard the rich man's
horse tramp by your dwelling, and sickened at the stony
gaze of the cruel rider. To think now, that half a hand-
ful from his heaps, would save me, and my boy, from
ruin. Oh, but he'll home to a dainty dinner! He
wants hunger to sharpen his appetite. See, how he
puts dish by dish from him, till his fancy's suited! And
mind ye, he cannot eat except from silver, or china.
Wretch! there's a fellow being, one of Heaven's creatures like yourself—as honest, as well fashioned, as
deserving—ay, more so—who starves for lack of that
ill-seasoned dish your palate despises. I could curse
thee!

EDITH.

Curse, did you say? Ah, Margaret! Calamity takes
many shapes sterner than poverty, and of these, be sure
a hard heart is the worst. The unpitying are the most to
be pitied. All is not ours that we have. We *possess* but
what we *enjoy*; and goodness is the spring of enjoyment. Thus the cruel may be called, of all, the poorest,
seeing they possess not what they have. The appetite
is sickly, the eye jaundiced, the heart withered; what
has been—a blank; what is—dissatisfaction; what is
to come—apprehension and hopelessness! Should such
a fate awake our curses?—or, our prayers?

MARGARET.

You are an Angel!

EDITH.

An Angel's hand would better serve you, than these few

coins from mine—take them, pray. But see, here comes
Master Lovel! (*She advances to meet* EUSTACE.)

MARGARET.

Dear young thing! Blessings be on her head. 'Twould
be a different world, an' there were many like her.

EDITH (*returning with* EUSTACE).

Joy! joy! Good news, Margaret! I dare not tell
you until I had sure grounds. Master Lovel has pleaded
your cause with Farmer Tilney, who will employ George
regularly, in his service.

MARGARET.

Is it true?   Is it true?   God reward your Honor!

EUSTACE.

And as for the few pounds of rent that you owe,—the
Squire will not be too hard, when he knows you will have
wherewithal to satisfy it.

MARGARET.

What will George say to this?   A thousand blessings
on you both.

EUSTACE.

There, there—you've said enough! 'Tis little an infirm body like myself can do; but what I can, I will.

MARGARET.

Ah, Sir!

EUSTACE.

Good night. Off with thee, to George! (*He rests on
a bench.*)

EDITH (*taking her hand*).

Good night, Margaret.

MARGARET (*with emotion*).

Good night—I needn't wish either of you happy
dreams, I fancy. (*She walks to the gate.*)

EDITH (*to* EUSTACE).

Alas! you seem weary.

EUSTACE.

Ay, lambkin! 'Tis all that I can do to hobble to
the town and home again. A short turn tires me now.
But no more of this. Hast thou written to Gerald?

EDITH.

I have, but 'twould grieve thee to hear how sadly.

EUSTACE.

Nay! I love all that thou writest. Pr'ythee read.

EDITH.

Thou shalt esteem my letter the child of a melancholy
hour which is past now. Come, then, to thine arm-
chair, which I have placed in the porch. (*They walk
to the porch of the Cottage.*) There's your throne;
your garden-kingdom there, and here your subject.
(*Placing herself on a cushion at his feet.*)

EUSTACE.

Now, Sweetheart!

EDITH (*reads*).

" Your latest letter, love, before me lies,
The source of many a care, and dark presage;
True—sorrow's record no more meets mine eyes,
Dejection casts no shadow on your page;
But ah! it breathes not hope. You shun the themes
That we were wont to love; but unsupplied
Their void remains, as if your early dreams
Fading, your very world had with them died.

" Oh! rather than this silence, would I hear
Grief's one-voiced current slowly wailing by;
'Tis hushed; but this still surface more I fear,
'Tis frozen, not becalmed—'tis apathy,

D 3.

And not content. I know how Misery stands
Alone, and doth companionship disdain ;
Yet, couldst thou see me kneel, and, with clasped hands,
Entreat the privilege to share thy pain,

" Would not the portals of thy heart unfold ?
It is *my home* they guard, and I should find
Its chambers in the darkness. Though the cold
Hath chill'd them, and for buried hopes, the wind
Chaunts mournful requiems ; though the dusky walls
Be draped with the dim 'scutcheons of the dead ;
Yet would I cry—' Dearer than festal halls,
The sacred, shrouded, solitudes I tread !'

" Gerald ! will you despair ? Though to achieve
A seeming greatness, you have vainly striven,
Yet *to be* great, is nobler : I believe
The Poet's fount of thought not chiefly given
That passing groups should praise its crystal stream ;
But his own human heart to fertilize—
A source of fruitful goodness—not a dream
Of transient beauty for admiring eyes.

" It may be both, I grant ; for e'en the *sight*
Of what is fair hath a refining spell ;
But if 'tis shunned of men, its own delight
Should in itself be found : in many a dell
Where trees o'ershade, and only zephyrs stray,
Bloom flowers of sweetest breath and loveliest hue
Unpraised—scarce pilgrims know that leafy way—
Only the stars their screen gaze kindly through.

" While sympathy the heart that else might break,
Can solace, or while hands the toil can share

Of the o'erburthened; while the lip can speak
Of truths eternal, and the region where
The evil no more trouble, and at rest
Are all the weary; while these tasks divine
Invite, what poetry may be expressed,
Although the poet never write a line!

" In him whom children love, whose serious talk
The village elders prize at evening's close;
In whose companionship a wonted walk
Rich with new meanings and fresh aspects grows,
Whose gracious influence ever intercedes
With man for man—the beautiful is *real ;*
His loveliest fancies shrine themselves in deeds,
And in his *heart* is guested his Ideal."

EUSTACE.

Read that again : I'm almost out of depth!

EDITH.

'Tis thus—that all he knows of right, he acts,
And all he deems is virtuous, would become.

EUSTACE.

Good, precious !

EDITH.

Are you easily reclined?
Stay, till I prop you with the cushion—so!

(*She resumes the letter.*)

" Wiser and sadder has my being grown
Since we beheld each other.   Ah, the change
The heart endures, chills not the heart alone,
But through the heart—the earth.   Whene'er I range

Our favourite haunts, although 'tis summer now,
And song is rife, tints warm, and Landscape fair;
I think that *thou* art sad—and fades the glow,
The music dies, and coldly strikes the air!

" Thy Father, Gerald—*mine* by love, indeed,
Entreats thee to return.   The staff of late—
His former plaything—hath become his need;
And less to walk, than sit, and meditate,
Inclines he now.   Your absence I am sure
Is all that irks him.   Dear Restorer, come!
His mind to brighter themes thy love shall lure,
And re-create for us, our long-lost home.

" I dreamed three nights ago—most precious dream!
The while I mused beneath the cottage eaves,
That through the rose-bush glorious light did stream,
And melody exhaled from all the leaves :
And then by gradual change the splendour took
A human aspect, and the music grew
Pregnant with thought—a voice!   Thine was the look,
The tones were thine—that thrilled my being through!

     *   *   *   *   *   *

" I laid my pen aside and stood alone
By the arched window, where we watched of yore
The Day-god on his slow descending throne
Of billowed radiance; or drew a store
Of precious fancies from each varying cloud
That played fantastic dramas in the sky,
Wild, but how beautiful—till twilight's shroud
In reverent stillness veiled the pageantry!

" The sight hath saddened me; my heart o'erflows
With these old memories; and the pleasant past,
The solemn future blend, and joys and woes
Before which speech retires—strange influence cast
Upon my spirit; but the thought of thee
Is central still, and with its charm endears
The ever fleeted hours; and tenderly
Tempers the bleakness of my coming years.

*   •   •   •   •   *

" Edith is calmer now.   'Tis true she looked,
And in her mirror marked with sad surprise,
What changes grief had wrought, and scarcely brooked
To think her altered face should meet thine eyes.
But then, *thy love* can make her spirit whole;
Though now cares wound, *with thee*, she could defy
      them;
And tears which down their self-worn channels roll,
She knows would vanish—didst thou come to dry
      them!"   (*After a pause.*)
Now think you he will come?

EUSTACE.

Heaven bless thee, child!
Thou lov'st that lad too well, sometimes, methinks,
Forgetting Him who holds at His control
All human hearts—to whom, in chief, are due,
Our faith and feelings, and whose love alone
Ne'er fails through weakness, ne'er deserts in woe,
Ne'er ebbs with waning fortune.   Cleave to Him
Whose power can work what man can only will,

Whose will is mercy, though its course be hid,
And issues in a grace beyond our prayers!

>   [*They enter the Cottage.*

SCENE.—*A richly furnished Room in* CLAYTON's *House
in Town. A profuse display of Pictures, Statues,
Vases, &c. &c.*

CLAYTON *and* GERALD.

CLAYTON.

Ashton speaks well of you; assures me that you are
well grounded in Italian, and that your French is that of a
Parisian. It were well, that to these acquirements you
could add the knowledge of Spanish and German.
Devote your leisure to them; and who knows that you
may not, eventually, transact our foreign correspon-
dence? That is, when time and care have familiarized
you with the requirements of so responsible an oc-
cupation.

GERALD.

I shall esteem it both my interest and my duty to
obey your instructions.

CLAYTON.

So far, so good!—But there is one maxim, Mr. Lovel,
I would impress upon your memory,—that in com-
merce, nothing is *unimportant;* and that no perfection
in what may appear its higher branches, can atone for
deficiencies in those which are seemingly inferior. Thus,
could you speak all the languages of Europe, did you
discover the shrewdest powers of calculation, or the
promptest wit in repairing an unforeseen misfortune—

I should still be dissatisfied, unless your invoice were written in a clear bold hand, and your entries made with precision and regularity. Upon the whole, diligence and patience stand a man in better stead than your more brilliant qualities.

GERALD.

To speak truth, my past course of life has been little consonant with the honourable avocations to which I shall henceforth devote it. I can but hope that you will bear with my necessary imperfections, and trust my desire to overcome them.

CLAYTON.

Frankly spoken! I like you all the more for this confession. (*More gravely.*) Yet there's one point to which I feel bound to allude—credit me, more for your future good, than from an unkind desire to recal your past errors—I have somewhere heard, perhaps from Ashton, that you have been addicted to tricks of idle rhyme, and wasted many valuable hours in spinning profitless vagaries of the brain. Now time, Sir, is money in this world. He who squanders time, is no less spendthrift than he who squanders gold. This must be altered—couplets, sonnets, odes entirely forsworn. Else, indeed, you might infect my clerks, disturb—nay, ruin—my whole mercantile economy!

GERALD.

Oh, Sir! Had Milton heard you.

CLAYTON.

What of him?

GERALD.

The toil of years, which rendered him immortal,
He sold for fifteen pounds!

CLAYTON.

There, my young friend,
You see what folly leads to.

GERALD.

And in truth,
None have more reason to regret the hours
Spent in these futile studies, than myself.
I vainly hoped to teach the world, forsooth!
And found the Author—his own Public.

CLAYTON.

The world has outgrown poetry. I'm glad
You thus discern your error, and avow it.
Nay, there's hope yet!   Good sense, and penitence,
Are earnests of reform.   But you look thin,
And very pale—a glass of wine?

GERALD.

No! no.
A few days will work mighty changes in me.
But what is this?   The mould of Hercules?
Here, Mercury with rod, and winged heel!
And here, a Claude—a very Claude, I swear!

CLAYTON.

Why stand you thus amazed?

GERALD.

Your pardon, Sir!
It were too bold to speak my thought.

CLAYTON.

Nay, speak!

GERALD.

You are a Father, and see not the danger!
Who e'er on earth beheld such godlike mould
As doth that marble show—or such a grace
As that fine attitude reveals?   The skies

That arch *our* isle, own no such glorious hues
As those the dreaming Artist hath pourtrayed
Upon this canvass.

CLAYTON.

How is this, young man—
Have you relapsed to your poetic flights?

GERALD.

No, surely! 'Tis but wonder you permit
These fanciful creations in your house!
May they not witch your daughters' hearts to pine
For forms, and scenes, which this good honest world
Holds rarely in its compass? And your Sons!
May not these fantasies distaste their minds
For love of actual life, and prompt desires
For occupations, pleasures, ends, and deeds
Such as your Poets fable? See you not
The peril you incur?

CLAYTON.

Fear not for me.
Mine's a well ordered household. For these prints,
And statues, they are fitting furniture,
And usual too, in modern drawing rooms—
We waste no thought on them, save as they fill
A vacant space with credit.

GERALD.

I protest
I'm yet scarce satisfied. I've suffered much,
And feel the danger keenly. Nay, I'd brook
No education, save what just avails
To make one's way in business. He who reads
French, or Italian, being England-born,
Must needs *imagine* France, or Italy.
That breeds desire to *see* them, warps the mind

This moment, did it please you.   Farewell, Sir,
Accept my thanks.

CLAYTON.

You shall hear further, soon.   [GERALD *goes out.*
I fear me, I can scarce admit this youth
To share my confidence.   His recent speech
Smacked much of Atheism!   Fie upon it!

THE WORLD.

PART III.

THE WORLD.

Scene. — *Hyde Park. The Ring thronged with Carriages and Horsemen.*

GERALD *and* ASHTON.

ASHTON.

Censure yourself! You reap but what you sowed.

GERALD.

The which, if all did—what scope would remain for Mercy? Mistake me not. The question is one of mere philosophical interest;—by no means designed as a plea, or argument, in mine own particular.

ASHTON.

Was I not your friend?

GERALD (*aside*).

Does Friendship, then, ever conjugate in the imperfect tense? (*Aloud.*) Very like ! What *is* a friend?

ASHTON.

A foolish specimen of philanthropy, that places its experience, counsel, and influence, at the disposal of another, and receives a sarcasm by way of acknowledgment.

GERALD.

A definition that in some degree accounts for the rarity of the species.

ASHTON.

Did I not remonstrate with you on the folly of your course? Did I not expose the fallacy of your notions,

and predict the lamentable issue of your infatuation?
Did I not, for your benefit, deduce from my own experience the maxims—I may say, the very *principia*—
of success? Did I not place in your way opportunity
after opportunity, for the promotion of your fortunes?
Did I not, in fine, use my interest in your behalf with
my worthy friend Clayton, at whose dearest prejudices
you took occasion to sneer? Good Soul! He took
your wit for blasphemy. And how often since, Mr.
Lovel, has this fine Ideal stepped between you and your
daily bread?

GERALD (*abstractedly*).

The world is all alike,—not that I blame it. I lost
my way at birth.—'Twas a mere accident; but an
irremediable one.

ASHTON.

For my part, I find no fault with the world. It
seems, bating a few necessary imperfections, a very
honest, cheerful, stirring, good sort of world. It has,
moreover, kind greeting for cordial hearts; although it
can return his own frown to the contemptuous caviller.
Ha! what do I see—my friend, Sir Harry Beverley?
So soon returned! A restive steed, that: So, gently!
I am somewhat pressed, Mr. Lovel! I trust that necessity will prove to you a more instructive preceptor
than I have been. My last advice—that of a friend,
believe me—is, that you should return to your country
home, and amidst the tranquillity of rural life, forget the
struggles and disappointments of your Metropolitan
career.

GERALD.

Farewell, Ashton! I have a vague feeling, which I
cannot well shape into words, that you might think

better of me, could you read my heart. Few know how deep a yearning for human love may lurk under the perverse satire that seems to repulse it. Believe me not wholly ungrateful—and again, farewell!

ASHTON (*taking* GERALD's *hand*).

Farewell! God bless you, Lovel! (*Aside.*) Now could I quarrel with myself for the lecture I gave him! No matter! The value of reproof sometimes consists in its harshness. (*They walk in opposite directions.*)

GERALD (*abstractedly*).

Great is this faculty of endurance. Our agonies derive something of mitigation from their very acuteness. The sense of pleasure may be palled by repetition. Why not, in like manner, the sense of pain? We may even lack the energy *to suffer*. Strange state, when our misery becomes the toy of our speculation! Oh, that from this trance there were no *awaking!* . . . . *Why needs there be?*

A BEGGAR.

Charity, charity, kind Gentlemen! Pray pity a poor old Soldier, who was wounded in the right knee at Waterloo, and obliged to limp on crutches for the rest of his days. Pray, Sirs, relieve my distress. May you never want the use of your limbs, kind Gentlemen! (*The crowd hurry by without regarding his importunities.*)

GERALD (*relieving him*).

Here, friend! I share my fortune with thee. (*Aside.*) Thou should'st have the other moiety, but that my need for it is even more urgent than thine.

A STRANGER (*to* GERALD).

Excuse me! From the readiness with which your

E

purse opens, I conclude you a novice in the tricks of
Town. A more infamous impostor than this pretended
cripple never rode from Bow Street at the Country's
expense. Sirrah—Look now! (*As the* BEGGAR *makes
rapidly off.*) That's tolerable speed for a cripple!
More the rascal merits iron round his wrists, than silver
in his palm. No offence, I hope, Sir? No offence,
I say? (*Passing on.*) Come! That's not what I call
the best of breeding. A civil question deserves some
sort of answer.

GERALD (*resuming his walk*).

" A very honest, cheerful, stirring, good sort of
world !"

SCENE.—*A more retired Part of the Park.*

ASHTON *and* SIR HARRY BEVERLEY.

SIR HARRY BEVERLEY (*dismounting, and giving his Horse
to his Groom*).

Not a word of apology! Thou shalt walk home with
me, Ashton, and dine from a dish of which Ude might
envy me the invention.—Let thine imagination take
its highest flight; I fear not that the reality will out-
soar it !

ASHTON.

In truth, Sir Harry, your past achievements have left
my fancy small scope for its exercise. Your present
effort must be indeed a *chef d'œuvre*, to distance its
predecessors !

SIR HARRY.

Why, thou doubter! Should not thy past ex-

perience of my powers, rather inspire confidence, than
scepticism ?

ASHTON.

Confidence were, indeed, the more philosophical mood;
since it secures, at least, the pleasures of anticipation.

SIR HARRY.

Truly, Ashton, my soul affecteth thee ! Thou art
one of the few men, who, having perpetrated a book,
yet candidly avow their *penchant* for the comforts of
this life.

ASHTON.

I esteem your dinner-giver the most practical of
philanthropists, and Gastronomy the key to all the
virtues.

SIR HARRY.

Solon might have profited by thy wisdom. And
now, most erudite Sage, indulge me by the develop-
ment of thy thesis.

ASHTON.

While the ideal of the Poet is altogether *prospective*,
and deals with a Future, which, how brilliant soever, is
incapable of realization ;—while the doctrines of the Philosopher, whatever their profundity,—nay, frequently,
on account of their profundity,—fail in the attainment
of a general and consistent embodiment ;—while the
machinery of Legislation is slow in its movements, and
in its results not once in a century touches the genuine
home-interests of mankind ;—while all these, I say, are
either limited, or futile in the amelioration of suffering,
or the induction of positive enjoyment ;—the *Dinner-
giver* does virtually communicate a tangible gratification, and confer a pleasure which, notwithstanding its
brevity, is certain, actual, and immediate !

SIR HARRY.

Oh, that I were a Stentor, to applaud thee !

ASHTON.

A well appointed dinner, unlike many inferior bene-
fits, excites a sense of gratitude without a sense of
obligation. The guest is no less essential to the host,
than the host to the guest. Each feels his mutual de-
pendence and reciprocal importance. Thus are strength-
ened the socialities of life; thus are fostered amiable
tempers, sparkling fancies, and benevolent emotions!
What feud so inveterate that the dinner bell will not
appease—or at least suspend it? To that soothing
sound yield friendly bickerings and family dissensions.
Concord reigns for the hour; and the household flag of
truce is unfolded—when the table-cloth is spread.

SIR HARRY.

Away, then, with those who denounce the Epicure,
as selfish !

ASHTON.

The gratified Epicure is the most charitable of men.
Depend on it the palate is one great avenue to the
heart; and that we never so sincerely compassionate
privations, as when we are the furthest removed from
their influence. Necessity, not *Ease*, is the occasion
of selfishness. False, indeed, was the dogma that we
become more accessible to the claims of Adversity when
we are ourselves the subjects of it.

SIR HARRY.

The authority of Dido, Queen of Carthage, is against
thee—

" Non ignara mali, miseris succurrere disco."

ASHTON.

Trust me, Æneas was more indebted to his *graces*,

than to his *misfortunes*, for the sympathy of the fair
Carthaginian.

SIR HARRY.

So nice a problem cannot be solved in a moment.
Perhaps the misfortune made the grace more charming;
while the grace rendered the misfortune more touching.
But, lo, Apsley House! Methinks my nostrils already
greet the odour of the *cuisine* in Clarges Street. Even
now do I observe my vespers with the accustomed
line—

> " May good digestion wait on appetite,
> And health on both !"—

To which request, if Ganymede be propitious, our eyes
shall be feasted after our palates. The Elsslers dance
to-night ! [*They cross the Park.*

SCENE.—*A small Apartment, meanly furnished.*

GERALD, LANDLADY, *and* LAURA, *a Child.*

LANDLADY.

I know 'tis a liberty, Sir; but I would warn you
against the soft, damp air, just before twilight. I'm
told that it's worse than an East wind to a delicate con-
stitution. Indeed, you give too little heed to yourself.
Had I my will, I would send for Doctor Donnington.
There's nothing like taking a complaint in time. That's
my maxim.

GERALD.

No need, good landlady. I shall secure the aid of
a tried Physician.

LANDLADY.

None of your new-fangled Quacks, I hope !

GERALD.

No! A Practitioner of marvellous skill, whose specifics are certain in their office, relieving when all others fail.

LANDLADY.

Deals he with any disease in particular?

GERALD.

With all cases, and with equal success in each—fever, madness, heart-ache! In fine, I know not the malady that can baffle his art.

LANDLADY.

Well, Sir! You're the best judge. Laura! Why, I declare, she's fastening a rose-bud in your button-hole. I have often to scold her for spending her few pence in such rubbish.

LAURA (*to* GERALD).

I wish Cinderella's were a true story! I wish there were good Fairies in these days! I know what I would ask of them.

GERALD.

Well, Laura?

LAURA.

Strawberry-cream, and a box of dominoes!

LANDLADY.

Heard one ever the like of that?

LAURA.

Stay! I would rather have a sackful of money.

GERALD.

Thou wert a strange child, else. And how would'st thou use it?

LAURA.

I'd give it all to you! Mother says you're very poor.

LANDLADY.

Laura, Laura !

LAURA.

You *did* say so, Mother; and that you must send
Mr. Lovel away; only when I cried so, you promised to
keep him.

LANDLADY.

Be still! Or look for a beating.

GERALD.

A beating!—She'll learn your lessons rapidly enough,
without the aid of correction.

LANDLADY.

You'll think nothing, Sir, of her foolish talk.   Out
with ye, hussy!   [LANDLADY *goes out, pushing*
LAURA *before her.*

GERALD (*after a pause*).

If Earth gain nothing by our lives, it shall lose
nothing in our deaths.   What, being had, is profitless;
being gone—costs no tears!   'Tis said now, that this
well-fashioned clay is not, after all, the true image, but
the mere mould of it !   Some have thought the essential
body pure ether—others have deemed it fire.   Fool!
what concerns it the world, whether thou be air, fire, or
a compound of all elements ?   What recks it who die?
They that live have their work to do.   Ages back, went
honest lamplighters their rounds at dusk ; and shall not
lamps be lighted on Doomsday eve ?   *   *   *   (*He
draws a phial from his bosom.*)

Mysterious Essence! potent Antidote
To thy great rival mystery—*Mortal Life,*
In name, and nature, equal paradox—
Strange is the love I bear thee, dallying

Like some tranced suitor in his wooing-time,
Content, though wedlock tarry. Courtship's well :
But marriage, better. Doubt not, Charmer Pale !
Hymeneal bonds are weaving. We shall wed
In the great pomp of Silence ! . . Nor ungraced
Shall pass our nuptials ; but the Slaves *within*,
Thralls of Necessity—the outworn powers
Yoked to Time's iron car, shall burst their chain,
And sleep, unfretted by the goad, or thong,
In memory of our bridals ! To your Rhines,
Your Italies, and your Helvetian Lakes,
Repair ere yet your dear illusions wane,
Ye mortal mates of Earth ! For *us* is moored
The barge of Charon, by the dreamy strand.
The Regal Pluto bids us to his feast ;
And thither by phantasmal shores we glide
In ghastly state—beneath an ebon sky—
O'er waves of rippling fire ! . . What ! dost thou
    chide
That I delay the pageant? Look, behold !
Thus do I pledge thee, Bride ! (*As he raises, with a*
    trembling hand, the phial to his lips, it falls,
    and is shivered to pieces.)
Alas ! that sound
Hath jarred all concord.

        Enter LORD ROXMORE.

    LORD ROXMORE (*advancing to* GERALD).
Do I speak indeed,
To Gerald Lovel ?

        GERALD (*mechanically*).
Yea. * * Just as I thought
To cast me on the bosom of the cloud,

The vague soft cloud below—did Time's cold gripe
Arrest, and drag me back.   The vision dies.
I wake to sense and suffering.

ROXMORE.

My name—
Roxmore—thou may'st have heard of, in the world?

GERALD.

At last, the world capitulates !   Away !
I spurn it utterly.   Its hour is past,
And mine is come !

ROXMORE.

Nay, suffer me !

GERALD.

Away !
Presume you so, Ambassador?

ROXMORE.

I know
You have borne much.

GERALD (*scornfully*).

The heart was once esteemed
A book—even Sages spelled in toil, and doubt;
But all men, now, can read it off at sight!
You know, forsooth !   (*In a low, hollow voice.*) Look
          at that hand !   Thou seest
'Tis frail, and thin ; and yet it would have wrenched
Jove's sceptre from his grasp.   *Doubtless, you know !*
And how, too, in requital of mine aim
His bolt my mounting pinion smote, and stretched
My racked frame at his feet, from whence I rolled
Adown his throne-steps, to the lowest round,
Where ebbs the fontal radiance.   But all this
Is stale *to your omniscience !*

E 3

ROXMORE.

Ambition!
Great is thy ruin here.

GERALD.

Ambition! right—
Euphonious lies have juggled us too long.
Ambition *is* ambition; and pride—pride!
Howe'er we gloss them o'er with softer names
Of aspiration, dignity, and so forth.
Ambition! true. Yet 'twas not alway thus.
Love once was mine—warm, gushing, happy Love!
It found no liberal course. The world's great dam
Repressed its flow, and then the waters *clomb*—
And that's Ambition—the recoil of love
On its own spring!

ROXMORE.

Canst thou be he whose lay
Hath ofttimes soothed us to delicious dreams—
Revived the fainting mind, and weary heart—
Whose lyre, like to the royal Hebrew's, breathed
Tones so harmonious, discord fled their sound?

GERALD.

What say'st thou?

ROXMORE.

That *thy life* hath bettered *mine!*
Have I not roved with thee through forest shades,
Hung with thee o'er the sounding cataract—
The avalanche of streams; or with thee sat
Beneath the leafy canopy of palms,—
Soared with thee to Thought's empyrean height,
Wept with thee in sweet pensiveness at eve;
And with thee, grown akin to all mankind?

GERALD.

It comes too late!

ROXMORE.

Not so; the Providence
That gave thee greatness, hath vouchsafed me wealth,
Bless'd, if it profit thee! What joy, methinks,
What honour, too, it were in Homer's scrip
But to have cast one mite!

GERALD.

Rest, only rest!

ROXMORE.

But, surely; error owned,
The truth revealed, the thought, and judgment clear,
The faculties yet vigorous—though impaired
By the frame's casual suffering that will pass
With these late vexing cares,—you nothing lack
That may assist your progress?

GERALD.

Only *will*.
I saw a Seraph lapsed from golden spheres,
Upon a kindless ridge of rock, alight.
Her pitying Sisters beckon her from high
To their primeval realms. She sadly smiles,
And points for answer, *to her broken wing!*

ROXMORE.

Nay! Change of scene will serve—

GERALD.

To change the soul?

ROXMORE.

Own'st thou no natural tie? Survive for thee
No tender Parent, no congenial hearts,
To share thy lonely grief? Or failing these—

No hallowed haunts of Childhood that might charm
Thy spirit from its sternness?

GERALD.

There, to find
Memory confront me with the Ghost of Youth,
And pointing to the shattered wreck I am—
Cry, " Such is Progress !" Oh, this Nature deals
In rare varieties ;—a worm converts
Into a beauteous voyager of air ;
And to fulfil her cycle—as you see,
Degrades ethereal being to the worm's !

(*The shades of evening have gradually increased, and
a soft, obscure light prevails in the apartment.
Lady Roxmore glides in unperceived by Gerald.*)

ROXMORE.

Yet answer me ! Though thoughts of good achieved,
The influence of change, the bonds of home,
The sanctity of memory—fail to soothe ;
Lives there for thee no form of grace, and love,
Bright as Romance's vision ; true as life,
The incarnation of thine own Ideal,
The shining substance of a dream as fair ?
Thou shalt not speak—not frowardly. Confess
That 'neath those names, and symbols in thy verse,
From old mythology, or fancy, drawn—
His *actual* did the Poet celebrate
In each melodious hymn !

GERALD (*sternly*).

Who gave thee right
To probe me thus ? Profanely, dar'st invade
The privacy of tombs ? For hearts are tombs

Where secret loves are buried out of sight,
And would'st thou scan them? Talking thus of tombs,
I had hoped, 'twas a moderate hope—to sleep
Under green earth, beneath a taintless sky,
In fair and wholesome quiet; and methought
I'd have a concave grave, with space for sound,—
High, wide, well scooped—that when at eve her feet
Pressed the adjacent turf, their cadent tread
Might my dark chamber with soft echoes fill!

ROXMORE.

Doth she not watch, and pray for thy return?
She saith—" He doth but tarry; he *will* come—
He'll surely come to-morrow!"

GERALD.

Oh, the realms
I swore to conquer for her! And all ends
In this maimed, baffled braggart's craving alms—
The dole of pity, and some hospital
Where may his wounds be tended!

LADY ROXMORE (*softly approaching* GERALD).
Hearken, now!

" Oh, in our days of early love, when from thy form,
    and face,
Exhaled an atmosphere of joy, and ever changing grace;
With sparkling eye, and braidless tress, and smoothed
    unshadowed brow,
Of every maid beneath the heavens, the brightest,
    blithest—*thou!*

" I prayed that not a tint of grief, or casual cloud of
    woe,
Might, o'er thy sunny stream of life, one darkening image
    throw;

But that, unvexed by storm, thy Time, with half-uncon-
    scious motion,
Might lapse into Eternity, as rivers into ocean !

" But, when thine hour of sorrow came, and every
    wounded feeling
Fled to my sympathetic love, for comfort, and for
    healing ;
Till sighs were hushed in thankfulness, and of the hand
    I press'd
The tremulous quivering testified how suffering might
    be bless'd !

" Bless'd—in the hidden mines of love, it opens to the
    day,
Bless'd—in the inner springs it moves, externally to
    play;
Bless'd—in the privilege it yields, of *trusting*, in our
    grief,
Bless'd—in the tenderness whose balm is dearer than
    relief!

" Then praised I Him who fashioned thus, these mystic
    hearts of ours,
Not merely for glad faculties, and all the smiling powers,
But for capacities of grief, and visitings of care,
Wherein Love claims prerogative—to solace, or to share!"

GERALD.

It must be ! Time is travelling backward !
       (*His eye falls on* LADY ROXMORE.)
Ah !
I deemed not thou would'st come.   It was not meet,
Fallen far from God, and Angels, I should stand

Within thy sanctuary.   But thou art here;
And we will part no more—*no more*, my love!
I will cling to thy robe, and at thy feet
Expire—if thou but move—How beautiful,
How exquisite thou art!—Yet changed withal;
Unto my sense, familiar, but unlike.
Pray, mock me not.—If thou be Edith, speak!

LADY ROXMORE.

Her messenger to bring thee to her sight!

GERALD (*rising*).

She'll marvel why we tarry,—let us hence!

LADY ROXMORE (*joyfully*).

At once!

GERALD.

I come, my love!   Fear not; I come!

RETURN.

RETURN.

SCENE.—*A Lane near the Country Town.*

YOUNG TOWNSMEN.

FIRST TOWNSMAN.

'Twas pity he did not close the good man's eyes.

SECOND TOWNSMAN.

When about to set forth on his journey hither,—(so run my tidings,)—a fever seized him.

THIRD TOWNSMAN.

Gerald, although he might not always hit it with worthy Master Eustace, was never, I believe, a bad Son!

SECOND TOWNSMAN.

From a chance sight of him, as I passed the garden gate, I fear he's travelling fast after his Father.

FOURTH TOWNSMAN.

His face flushed?

SECOND TOWNSMAN.

No; but pale in a strange sort.

THIRD TOWNSMAN.

Pale's pale man! Are there two sorts of pallor?

SECOND TOWNSMAN.

Two, at least, as I will prove to thee. Last spring, the Squire and his family being away, by favour of my Cousin, the Steward, I was let to wander over the grounds.—You remember my Cousin Farleigh. He

knows all the Squire's private matters, and would
astonish many in our town, told he all he *could!*

FOURTH TOWNSMAN.

Ay, ay! We know thy Cousin. 'Twere no fault
of thine did we forget him. But now to thy story.

SECOND TOWNSMAN.

Well! What I thought best worth seeing in the
Squire's gardens, and what I best remember—are the
Heathen Statues that one pops suddenly upon, at every
other turn in the walks. Gad, Sirs! These stone
men were chalked after a good pattern. There was
one bold muscular fellow, just cut out for a wrestler;—
I would scarce tackle his like at fair time. But the
young women—I'm speaking of their images—beat all
I ever set eyes on. They made a complete fool of me.
My eyes piped—I an't ashamed to confess it—when I
thought such shapes and faces were only dead stone.

FIRST TOWNSMAN.

Gad! Being flesh and blood, they had given thee
more cause for tears. I should say, a pretty lass carved
in stone was the perfection of beauty—All its charms,
and nought of its mischief.—But thou forgettest
Gerald!

SECOND TOWNSMAN.

Not at all. I stayed in the grounds till after sunset.
Twilight came on, quite unawares. I was an hour out
in my reckoning. The moon rose without making me
the wiser, till I was startled to see its silver gleam
thrown full on one of the marble faces. Note, it was
not yet dark, the moon was large, white, and near the
Earth!

FIRST TOWNSMAN.

Well! Of Gerald?

SECOND TOWNSMAN.

I never saw two things more alike, than his face and
that statue's, in the cold glitter of the moon.

FOURTH TOWNSMAN.

And didst thou go so round-about a way, to possess
us of this fancy?

SECOND TOWNSMAN.

Fancy?

FOURTH TOWNSMAN.

Ay, truly!   What else canst thou make of it?

SECOND TOWNSMAN.

There are many things real enough of their kind, that
pass words to explain them.

FIRST TOWNSMAN.

Poor Gerald!

THIRD TOWNSMAN.

I always thought he had a good heart.

SECOND TOWNSMAN.

What we called scaliness, was but his way.

FOURTH TOWNSMAN.

Ay!   Or suppose he *had* faults, who's without 'em?

(*Scene closes.*)

SCENE.—*A Pathway bordering the Fields.   The Spire
of a Church in the Distance.*

GERALD *and* EDITH.

EDITH.

Doth not thy spirit from these peaceful scenes
Draw restoration, solace, beauty, rest?

GERALD.

Ah! Nature can reproach, as well as soothe.
To her may Virtue from the world repair,
For health, and consolation,—nor in vain.
For in her youth perpetually renewed,
Procession calm, and unsuspended life—
Is symbolised the tranquil might of Love,
And Truth's serene immutability.
Thus, still, by holier minds the type is hailed
As earnest of a human altitude,
Hereafter to be won.   But idly *here*
Shall vexed Ambition or worn Avarice court
Repose and vigour.   In their order due
The plains resume their verdure, and the hills
Still turn their wonted aspects to the skies !
Still planets keep their trysting time with Earth !
Still Ocean laves the shores, and emulates
The rock-tower with his billow !   Constant Day
Still wakes the world which the unfailing Night
Still kindly wins to slumber—as though ne'er
Lean, quivering hands had piled enjoyless hoards,
Or the long crash of falling thrones disturbed
Rapt Nature's heaven-bound ear.   Oh ! he alone,
May seek in Time for solace, who can look
Beyond it, for his bliss.   (*He turns into the pathway
leading to the Churchyard.*)

EDITH.

Not *there* to-night.   I know thy filial love
Tends to our Father's grave, where, eve by eve,
Thy vigils have been passed.

GERALD.

Best let the heart
Have its own way, and what it failed to learn

From living worth—read sadly at the tomb. (*They walk
on in silence, until they enter the Churchyard.*)

GERALD (*pausing*).

Yes! Here he sleeps. My Father! dear, dear Father!

EDITH.

He was an upright, loving, humble man.

GERALD.

He was, he was! and every day that saw
My youth expand, should in my heart have fed
The fervent love I owed. I should have been
His chief companion, constant minister
To every wish—shared all his quiet joys,
Aided his kindly spirit, ever fain
To make all round him happy. But, alas!
I deemed myself too great for such mean ends—
Played Critic, and not Brother, to the world!
Our Life's affections are its sanctity,
Its vestal fires! Should *they* die out, albeit
In the Mind's Temple every niche doth boast
An intellectual glory—still the pile
Loses its holiness—is desecrate!

EDITH.

But surely thou hast taught this in thy page!

GERALD.

Oh! that my page had taught it to my heart.
How much of self was mingled with my aims.
I would have blessed the world—dowered it with light,
And joy, and beauty.—Ay! but then the world
Must know *I* bless'd it. Pitiful! and vain—
Diseased at core! I think at God's great bar
There will be fewer *evil deeds* condemned,
Than good deeds for ill ends!

EDITH.

What ! Deem'st thou Sin—
The hope of Fame ?

GERALD.

I say not that.   His heart
Lacks a fine chord—that thrills not to the touch
Of Human gratitude !   To strike the rock
Till crystal waters gush ; and with the wand
Lay bare the hidden treasures of such earth
As sterile looks at surface—to do this,
And *to be known to do it*—yields delight.
Conscience forbears to challenge.   But to prize
The praise we win more than the good we work,
Yea, to compare the two in worth—degrades !
The truly great are *fashioned* so, and shed
Their affluent beauty round—as planets shine,
Birds sing, and rivers roll from laws within,
From native impulse, elemental life !
Their origin, their motive—is above ;
And nought below, compels them—or restrains.

EDITH.

Are such exempt from suffering ?   Boast they hearts
Mailed 'gainst the scoffer's sting, or brutal shaft
From the coarse curve of Hatred's lip discharged ?

GERALD.

Speaks gentle Edith thus ?   No ! no ; the soul
Heaven's love inspires—is vulnerable still;
But such its nature's virtue, never wound
There *rankles*—Tho' the barb's keen *smart* be felt—
Its *poison* is repelled.

EDITH.

Strangers approach !

GERALD.

I will not hear that word. No man, to-night,
Can be a stranger, Edith!

EDITH.

These are friends!
Look! They observe thee, and retreat—perchance
Fearing they should intrude upon thy grief.

GERALD.

We'll speak to them. (*Advancing*.) Fair even to you,
    friends!

FIRST TOWNSMAN.

Most welcome to your home! For his dear sake
Whom we would claim to mourn—almost as children—
Accept our love.

SECOND TOWNSMAN.

We never shall forget him!
His counsels kind, and wise—the willing help
He lent in every need—awake regret
As for a parted Father!

FOURTH TOWNSMAN.

He is gone.
Ne'er shall we see his like!

THIRD TOWNSMAN.

Nay! nay!—I trust
One good man's death not quite exhausts the world.
    (*In a lower voice to* GERALD.)
Mayhap my boldness says it—but methinks
In sweet Miss Edith, all his virtues live;
The self same air—set in a softer key!
You've seen how she is worshipped, hereabout;—
Her deeds a treasured theme in every hut,
Her name upon the lip in every prayer!

F

GERALD.

I know her all you say.   (*Aside.*) Ah, would that I
Had in my retrospect as fair a life !

FIRST TOWNSMAN.

Now, pray be charier of your health !   'Tis late
For one so delicate, to be abroad.
Farewell ! We wish you both a kind good night,

GERALD.

Farewell, good Friends ; and thanks !
(*They exchange salutations, and the Group passes on.*)
I scorned ye once !

EDITH (*after a pause.*)

Shall we not follow, Love ?   The dews descend.

GERALD.

A little longer yet.—Oh ! I could muse
Until my soul exhaled in tender thought !
How *can* men hate each other ?   While I stand,
Graves at my feet, and but the sky above,
Suggestive Nature whispers sympathy ;
And in the presence of two common homes—
One for the flesh, and for the spirit one—
Asks—" Are ye not all Brethren ?"

EDITH.

True !—Could men live with Death before their eyes,
How changed would be their bearing.   Many a word
Of harsh repining, many a scornful look—
Would be unsaid, unworn !   (*They walk slowly on.*)

GERALD.

And, after all
Our years of study, shrewd conjecture, quest
Of philosophic oracles—to hear
At last, Truth's touching accents in these scenes
Of common, simple pathos ! (*Pausing.*) See ! There sleeps
The Lady of the Manor.

EDITH.

She whose name
Yet lives in grateful memories?

GERALD.

The same.
'Twas in my childhood, still delight to watch
Her pure, pale face!   A hapless lot was hers—
Mated by this world's policy to one
In nature harsh, and proud; in carriage stern.
Her life was one of trial—meekly borne!
So meekly—that *her* voice alone withheld
Its witness to her wrong.   And still her days
Were spent in blessing others, as her love
Had drawn new motive to heal foreign grief,
From that was native to her.   'Twas a prayer
Of prudent beauty that she breathed ere death—
To rest beneath the open sky, beside
Those lowly ones whose lives her bounty cheered,
Whose hopes she fostered, and whose pangs she soothed!
Oh! better far for Resurrection's morn
To find her thus, among the grateful poor,
Whose lips shall vouch in her behalf to Heaven—
Than 'neath the stateliest Mausoleum's roof
Man ever reared to keep his dust select!—
I ask not why; but in this last half hour,
Methinks, I have become a child again!

EDITH.

He who best knew the heart, did He not say
Heaven's kingdom was of Childhood?   Dearest Gerald!
Does it not seem, when tender musings steal
Over our human feelings, in best hours,
As though our souls turned magnet-like to Christ,
And owned celestial affinities,
Making them vibrate, trembling to His truth?

F 2

GERALD.

Oh! THOU whose sacred name by countless lips
Is day by day adjured; on whom relies
The world for mercy—grant thy *spirit*, Lord!
We trust thy death—conform us to thy life!
THOU who wert found at Cana's feast—a guest,
Whose tears were shed by Lazarus' lowly tomb,
Whose grace absolved the Malefactor's sin
When by thy Cross he hung—the scorn of men!—
Whose failing voice—*Forgive them, Father*—cried!
May we like thee, in every guileless joy
Our genial part sustain, like thee confess
The obligations dear of human ties,
By thee instructed, cherish kindly faith
To all who wear the form which thou didst wear;
And quit the world with mercy on our lips—
Most meet for those who hope their all from *thine!*

EDITH.

My heart responds—Amen!
      (*They pass through the gate of the Churchyard.*)

GERALD.

See—The high-road!
'Tis the more cheerful way.   What sounds are those—
Blithe, stirring, lively, such as youth might tread
A measure to, in May?

EDITH.

It is the voice
Of Robert's violin—the blind Musician—
Would he had tuned it to a sadder strain!

GERALD.

Oh! why should there be sadness— where not guilt?

REST.

REST.

SCENE.—*The High-road.*

The VILLAGE PHYSICIAN *on horseback, and* FRANKLIN,
*an elderly Yeoman—engaged in Discourse by the
Gate of a Corn-field.*

PHYSICIAN.

Truly, friend, all men are mortal! Yet hath this
mortality no *certain* premonitions. I have known
Death's door creak on its hinges, without opening wide
enough for passage; and again that very door has
opened so suddenly, you would not have guessed it,
but for the clang of its shutting. But how chances
harvest to be still unhoused? Your sickles have been
busy these three weeks.

FRANKLIN.

Why, Sir, we've waited for the backward corn.
Some ears take to the sun earlier, and more kindly than
others. In the same field, shall you find mingled the
golden spike—and the green; the firm—and the soft;
the ripe—and the sprouting. But, as to my old friend
Lovel's Son, can't you speak more to the purpose,
Doctor?

PHYSICIAN.

Men *have* recovered with whom it went yet harder.

FRANKLIN.

But barring miracles, and judging by likelihood—
'tis a bad case, I fear.

PHYSICIAN (*shaking his head*).

I fear so; but Heaven knows its appointed time.
If that be *not* come, the Patient may defy Disease,
whether chronic or acute. Pulmonary Consumption,
Affections of the Heart, Scarlet Fever, and Ague;
Epilepsy, and Apoplexy—cannot touch life, until the
hour be come—and *then*, a stream of air passing through
half-open doors, or the chink of ill-closed windows,
does Death's bidding with despatch, and completeness.

FRANKLIN.

I watch my vine daily. One more week's sun, and
the grapes may be gathered. Though but English
grapes, the fruit of them may not be ungrateful to a
sick palate. I wait but their ripening to visit Gerald.
For his Father's sake, though the way be far, I must
look on the dear lad's face, once again in this world.

PHYSICIAN.

Tarry not, good Franklin, for the ripening of the
grape.

FRANKLIN.

Think ou his end so near? Poor lad! I can remember him, since he was *that* high!

PHYSICIAN.

We've all grown older since then.

FRANKLIN.

True, Sir! In the bit of garden, at back of my
house, many's the pipe-bowl dear old Lovel and I have
emptied together in the cool of the evening: while the
little 'un—Mister Gerald as is now—in white pinafore,

and straw hat, would be horsing my stick. I could almost swear to seeing his brown ringlets just now waving about his white shoulders. How fond was my Bess of playing with them long brown ringlets! She couldn't have been prouder of the boy, had he been her own. But she's gone—my dear Bess!

PHYSICIAN.

She's where I trust we're all going, Franklin!

FRANKLIN.

I shall never forget the first harvest-home after I lost her. According to custom, the men and lads assembled in the barn to take their lunch of cake and their cup of ale, and to finish the business with three roof-shaking cheers. Now, Bess, you see, had been used at these times to come into the barn, and pledge the labourers with me; and faith, when I carried my jug to my lips, I turned round, as natural-like, expecting to see her, as though she had not lain three months in her grave! Remembering *that*, I well nigh choked; and at first, when the men cheered, I could have struck them to the earth for mocking me. But I soon came to my right mind, and shook hands with each, and all, as though nothing had happened. . . And how takes poor Miss Edith her lover's sickness?

PHYSICIAN.

I've not seen Miss Fairlie these three weeks. By some hap or other, she's ever absent when I call. I can't understand it; she used to be so fond of a chat with old Doctor. I don't wonder now, however, at the store she sets by Gerald. He's half an Angel already.

FRANKLIN.

Knows he of his danger?

F 3

PHYSICIAN.

At his special instance, ere I rode forth, I possessed
him with my apprehensions of the worst.

FRANKLIN.

What said he?

PHYSICIAN.

He smiled, and thanked me. But to reach Rochfort
Court ere night-fall, I must needs push on. God be
with you, Master Franklin!

FRANKLIN.

As with you, Sir! A pleasant ride.

SCENE.—*An Apartment in* GERALD's *Cottage.*

GERALD (*alone*).

" *This world is not your rest;*"—words surely writ
Not to disparage earth, or disaffect
The mind to temporal action; not one link
That binds humanity in love, to rend,
Not one of life's endearments to dissolve,
So they be pure; nor from Creation's stores
Of varied beauty, to diminish aught,
Or aught depreciate; but that we should count
This brief existence to the Land of Rest
A pathway, shortening, every step we take.
Or, as the voyager to some glorious isle,—
His natal region, bound,—waves greeting kind,
Whene'er the winding shores some charm disclose;
Or on the bleaker coast smiles patiently—
So should we pass through Time,—our ruling care
That we secure our Father's " Welcome Home!"
And yet 'tmay be forgiven that we lament

Some friend, or sister—our companion long,
At the last port detained, and in our wake,
Not by our side, to sail. Sweet Edith! Mine
Must be the task, to this division brief,
Thy will to reconcile, which still denies
Its credence to the Fate that severs us.

Enter EDITH.

She comes—in smiles, too!

EDITH.

Read!

GERALD.

A newspaper!

EDITH.

Yes—to thy greatness, Man, at length, awakes!
A genial mind here echoes to thy song.
Mark how this noble spirit—like to one
Who in the wilderness some fount espies,
And with the tidings to his comrades hastes—
Proclaims thy new found beauty to the world!

GERALD.

Join me in praise to Heaven, whose omens speak
My life not wholly fruitless. Laud we Him
Who ne'er his creatures gifts with faculties
Of Light, and Beauty, but for final use.
His Chosen their allotted tasks fulfil;
Their individual errors are atoned
In their own fate. The seeds of Truth they sow
For selfish glory—are still sacred seeds,
And bear their righteous fruits for general weal,
When sleeps the Husbandman beneath their shade!

EDITH.

There's sadness in thy thought—

GERALD.

Solemnity;
But not a tint of sorrow.   All is peace.

EDITH.

How have thy trials sanctified thy soul.
Oh, in our coming days, when health renewed,
Sheds vigour through thy frame; when stirring life
Reclaims thee to its service, and thy pen,
Thy lip, thy hand—their offices resume—
What morals wrought in suffering, wilt thou teach.
What truths from tribulation learned, unfold!

GERALD (*aside*).

Still to that dream she clings.   (*Aloud.*) It has pleased
        Heaven
Much to reveal that was erewhile obscure,
Much to illumine that before was dark,
Much that was drear to brighten.   Bend thy glance
On yon still plain of graves; that lone churchyard
My fancy once had peopled with the shapes
We draw from *Memory*.   Now with forms of *Hope*
'Tis haunted to my vision.   Why should Dread,
And Cheerless Anguish by the portals sit
That ope on Immortality?

EDITH.

Wherefore
'Tis thus, I know not—ask not; but *it is*.
To part from the familiar is a pang—
How much more, from the good!

GERALD.

We must lament:
It is the proper weakness of the heart.
Yet, still should patience, faith, humility,
Our very sense of chastisement, chastise.

The virtuous should be mourned by virtuous deeds,
More than by tears.   The holiest memory
Embalms the image of the pure, *in life,*
And tunes the mourner's spirit to the charm
Of Beauty he deplores; even as the Skies
At day's decline shroud not their brows, but strive
By funeral torches kindled for the Sun
To emulate his ministry of Light.

EDITH.

Come, shall we move?   This northern prospect wears
A bleak stern look.

GERALD.

Thou dost the landscape wrong,
Capricious one!   I've heard thee oft commend
Yon valley's shadowed calm, and bless the spire
Round which the hills in natural fealty rear
Their guardian ramparts.

EDITH.

Call me fickle, Love!
Perverse, or what thou wilt; but humour me.
Come to the quaint, arched lattice, that o'erlooks
Our little garden—There! the curious screen
Of glass wrought in a hundred diamond panes
Flies open from its frame.   The freshening tide
Of fragrant air pours in.   Hush! list awhile
The insect hum below.   There! look—that bee
From our frail sickly rose-bush hath emerged
Laden with nectar.   Charitable bee!
That from the stunted, and forsaken shrub,
Can yet draw sweetness!

GERALD (*aside*).

Is it chance alone,
Or some strange instinct in her heart that shuns

The theme I would discourse of?   (*Aloud.*) Dost thou
    know
The kind Physician—

            EDITH (*interrupting*).

Yes! I watched him go,
'Tis full three hours since.   He rode briskly off,
A picture to behold !   His figure staid
And heavy in the formal garb attired,
A century old in fashion, and the hat
Grave and broad-brimmed that overhung his eyes—
With his slight, frisking nag such contrast wrought,
As must have moved your laughter !

            GERALD.

Edith !

            EDITH (*rapidly*).

Well,
I was about to say, to Rochfort Hall
He briskly rode, anticipating night.
Do you remember Rochfort Hall ?—the rooms
With their dim tapestry, and legends old,
The lonely galleries, and that dark gaunt knight,
Whose portrait heads the stair.

            GERALD.

Edith !

            EDITH.

E'en now
In thought I oft the lineaments recal,
Pensively beautiful, of Lady Grace—
Proud Rochfort's heiress—who, her lover slain,
For that, she could not brook familiar scenes
He might no more revisit—disappeared
Without or sign, or trace—beyond the seas
To find a nameless grave.

GERALD.

Before me, too,
A distant journey lies—

EDITH.

Not yet! not yet!—
Thou must be cautious, patient; nor presume
Too soon on growing strength.

GERALD.

Mine own beloved!
Thou wilt be patient, too, while I disclose
What from my kind Adviser's lips I learned
Ere his departure.

EDITH.

Yes! I wait.—What said he?

GERALD.

What if he say that in a blander clime,
Where southern breezes, rife with balm, prevail,
My days must henceforth pass—what if he say
That my mind needs congenial themes, must seek
The groves of Antique Song, and muse amid
The graced memorials of old Roman power.—
The tombs of Heroes, Sages, Senators—
What is thine answer?

EDITH.

We will go, my Love!

GERALD.

But what if I must go in solitude;—
Say for some special reason, undivulged,
With thy dear presence part—perchance for years?

EDITH.

Why am I not thine own, thy plighted one?
He would not bid us part!

GERALD.

Yet did he name
Such harsh condition, what would'st thou elect?—
Should I remain?

EDITH.

At peril of thy life?
No! Go—I trust thee; I could die for thee!

GERALD.

I go, beloved! But not to Southern Climes,
For even *there* is tempest.   I depart,
And for a realm where peerless glories reign;
Where Sages, Poets, Potentates are throned!
Not to their tombs; but to their homes I go.
The lore they teach is Truth; the hymns they chaunt
Are to God's praise; the crowns that wreath their
     brows
Are fadeless—woven from the Tree of Life!

EDITH.

Ha! The cloud bursts at last; and blasts the bolt—
The bolt that spares to kill!

GERALD (*apart*).

I scarcely deemed
This blow would fall so sternly.

EDITH (*bursting from him, and wildly traversing the
room*).

Cruel Death!
That hears not intercession.   Sternest hearts
Have erst been melted by a woman's tears;
But *He* hath no relentings.   Pitiless!
Untouched by beauty of the thing he slays—
The world that claims it, and the one whereto
It is *itself*—THE WORLD.   Oh, Coward Death!

Who takes no shape that we may wrestle with—
But deals his blow in darkness!

GERALD.

Cease! Forbear.
The peace I deemed in my Soul's centre fixed—
Rocks at thine awful words. Would'st thou arraign
The Lord of Death and Life, who, when He takes,
As when He gives, is bless'd—in both Divine?
Or would'st thou dim my closing hours with grief
At thy mistrust—thy madness?

EDITH.

Dost thou love?

GERALD.

Ay;—but my love is lofty, as befits
One on Death's threshold. Do I love thee? Yes—
Yes, Edith! but my love may not *descend.*
It bids thine—*soar!*

EDITH (*falling at his feet*).

Oh! pity, and forgive.
I am not worthy thus to clasp thy knees—
So godlike thou—so frail, and guilty I.
Yet, think what 'tis to lose thee—my Soul's centre!
The Past is but another name for thee!
To take thee from the Future—takes its light,
Its motive, vigour, interest,—all that makes
Life more than stagnant Time. Oh, spurn me not—
Unto my wretchedness impute my sin,
And pardon, if thou canst no longer love!
Alas! the death, to outlive hope.

GERALD (*tenderly*).

Rise! rise!
Hope ne'er deserts the heart that holds to Virtue.

Let trial follow trial; wealth decrease,
Privation humble.   Let the cherished dreams
That thronged youth's Future pass, as golden hues
From the horizon dissipate, and die
In cold, blank night;—Change scatter o'er the globe
Love's covenanted band—till all outworn
We roam like exiles on the shores of Time,
And from its dim sepulchral confines catch
Brief, fitful glimpses of receding souls
Entering the shadow of the Infinite,
And reckless of our prayers;—still Hope consoles,
And bids us trace, across the deep of Death,
Her rainbow's outline, faint—but perfect still!

EDITH.

One word—Believ'st thou in those brighter spheres
Whereto we tend, Soul may remember Soul?

GERALD.

Oh doubt it not.   The Maker takes the name
Of Father; Christ—of Brother.   In that Realm
Shall all the blest relationships survive
Of kindred, and of friendship.   The Divine
Is human nature hallowed,—not destroyed.
Hence, in a Mother's blessing, in the love
That mingles Soul with Soul, and in the bonds
That man unites to man, we but fulfil
Eternal Laws of kind, and brotherhood.
There, even there—may Spirits recognise
The ties on earth deemed sacred.   There perchance
With filial gratitude may sons recal
The counsels, and the tenderness of Sires!
There they whose lives were blended, may invite
Sweet retrospects of many a mutual aid—

The smile that banished fear, the faith that shone
So clear through trial, that they blest the night
For the dear star that brightened in its gloom!
There, in their equal affluence may steal
Over the poor man's memory the boon
His pitying brother granted! There the throng
The brave redeemed from vassalage, may gaze
With conscious love on the Deliverer's brow!—
All that is good in Earth, endures in Heaven:
'Tis the alloy that fades. Ah! There, no more
Shall chance or death divide, or age subdue;
Or treachery wound, or passion stain—the soul!
No vice, no weakness in the breast we love
Shall wake our tears, or chill our trust! No more
Shall misconstruction sadden earnest hearts;
Or the dull sensual jeer, or apathy
Freeze the soul's fount of feeling! There dwells mind
Than youth more buoyant, more mature than age;
There Hope is Prophecy; there Fancy dies
Merged in the actuality of Bliss;
And there is Wisdom, Love; and Love is Life!

EDITH.

Oh blessed words! The cheering theme resume.

GERALD.

Can they be desolate, who know that Heaven
Counts in its shining ranks their parted friends?
Is it not sweet to deem immortal eyes
Bend o'er us, in the myriad walks of life;
Mark all the suffering borne, the duty done,
The blessing granted, and the wrong forgiven?
What joy to feel the love that would aspire
To God—attracted in its upward course

By every human agency which *here*,
Too oft would lure the mounting soul to Earth!
How holy, how ennobling,—to reflect,
That by our natural ties, our fellowships
Owning their source in Time, we stand relate
To sainted souls, and 'mid Celestial Hosts
May claim a parent, partner, child, or friend!
And thus, the ransomed just have privilege
To lend new aids to Heaven, and in degree
Partake the virtue of that Holiest One
Who conquered Death, in dying; from whose grave,
As from a quarry, pillars luminous
Were hewn to bear the dome of Mercy up!—
Ah, Edith mine! by all our memories,
By all our mutual hopes, and blended fate,
By thine own love which in my darkest hour
Held ope the portal through which Pity past
To this despairing spirit,—let thy soul
With mine, some token of its peace exchange.
See! The Sun lingers on the horizon's verge,
As he were loath to bid the world—good night,
Till thou and God were reconciled!

                         EDITH.

Go! go!
I would not keep thee from thy Home of Light—
Where the voice calls thee—go! and I will bless it.

              GERALD (*sinking on a chair*).
As I do thee!

                         EDITH.
A change comes o'er thy voice!

              GERALD (*softly*).
I know not if it be the light *within*

That by its emanation doth imbue
The externe with radiance, or the wonted mood
Of tenderness approaching farewells bring,
In which old jarrings, and discordance die,
And with our parting grasp we all forget,
Except our friends' good offices—but now,
Only Time's fairest aspect meets mine eye,
And Earth's meek Angel with my spirit pleads
To bless the star she sways—the Vestibule
In which, though scarce distinctly, one might catch
The sacred cadence of the Temple's hymn.
(A pause.)
Methinks I hear it now, so full, so clear,
One might almost believe the solemn gates
Unfolded for its issue.   O'er my frame
Delicious languor steals. . . . Dost thou not deem
The shadows lengthen rapidly to-night?

EDITH.

Ah me! thy voice floats like a dream of sound,
A sigh of superhuman melody!
Thou shalt have rest—I will not speak with thee

GERALD.

Go, Love! and tell me whether yet the ray
Gild the horizon's line.   (She goes to the window.)

EDITH.

'Tis visible;
But vanishing.

GERALD (faintly).

I felt it.   So we pass.—
Father!—To Thee this dear one . . I commend.
Silence . . . is music, now! . . . . Edith! (Dies.)

EDITH (*from the window*).

'Tis gone!   (*She approaches* GERALD.)

Gerald!—*My Gerald!* (*An interval of subdued
        weeping.   She sinks on her knees by his side.*)

STILL, THY WILL BE DONE.

THE END OF GERALD.

POEMS.

POEMS.

THE TWO FAITHS.*

A MANSION old, with regal air,
 And veteran trees on either side
Standing like true adherents there,
 In honoured age, and loyal pride!
In front, a lake outspread—that wore
 A ceinture soft of bosky green;
And on its breast an Islet bore,
 Whence rose, in solitude serene,

A meek and venerable pile—
 Gentle its mien, but stately too;
Around, the sweet yet solemn smile
 It shed, that virtuous Elders do.

---

* The following lines were occasioned by a little narrative which I heard some years since. It appears that the union of a highly gifted and fondly attached pair, trained up in the Roman Catholic faith, was for ever precluded, by the secession of the gentleman to the Protestant Church—an event which occurred almost on the eve of their anticipated nuptials. A sad and final farewell ensued; the affection and esteem of neither being diminished, but subordinated by both to what they esteemed the obligations of Conscience.

Through storied panes the sunbeams fall
   On sculptured knights with claspéd hands ;
And 'mid two dream-like arches, tall,
   Like Rest, the mild Madonna stands.

Ah! moss-grown porch, and silver lake,
   And tranquil isle—it seems unmeet
Your imaged beauty should rewake
   Long dormant woes.   With all replete
Are ye—that charms the heart, and eye ;
   But since the hour that reft my fate
From her's with whom ye welcomed me,
   Deserts would seem less desolate !

We truly loved.—It was the change
   Of Faith, that pointed paths apart.
A difference that could scarce estrange
   The long-linked feelings of the heart.
We bade adieu—as those who mourn
   Ties rent by *Fate*—not *Will*—in twain ;
We parted—never more to turn
   Our steps to that meek Islet-fane !

And since that hour, mine ear no more
   Hath caught the tones—its music then ;
And all that gilded life before,
   Hath never brightened it again !
Yet, still, at musing twilight hours
   My thoughts to her will often roam ;
Strays she by streams, or rests in bowers—
   Such as of yore adorned her home ?

I wonder, when the roses blow,
  If one more happy than the rest,
Contrasts its crimson with the snow
  Of her unspotted, virgin breast.
I wonder, when the balmy dews
  O'er the still landscape softly steal;—
If they into *her* heart infuse
  The thoughts which, while they sadden—heal!

And there be times when to mine ear
  The lips of strangers breathe her name;
'Tis marvel I should seldom hear
  Of her whose praises all proclaim!
" I thought you were acquainted !—No ?"
  " In gone-by years I may have met her."—
" But 'twere impossible, I know,
  If that had happened—to forget her !"

No ! I forget not. And whene'er
  Before our Father's throne I bend—
I seek, with many a streaming tear,
  His favour for that early friend;
And thank Him, though my lot denies
  My heart in any other way
To manifest its sympathies—
  I yet have liberty—*to pray !*

JOY AND SORROW.

Sorrow and Joy! Ye that appear
So contrary—the one austere;
The other soft and mild—
Ye spring from one paternity,
The twin-begot of Deity;
And each he calleth child.
Joy ever cheereth me, when I
Dwell with his Father, God;
And to mine ear come Sorrow's sigh,
When I go forth abroad,
Seeking, in outward shadows dim,
The light that dwells alone in Him.
Thus both the same high lesson teach,
Apostles that one moral preach;
Joy ever wooing me to stay
With Him whose smile sheds constant day;
And Sorrow crying, when I roam—
" Celestial—Earth is not thy home!"

THE LAUREL AND THE ROSE.

" Oh what is like me?" said the Laurel tree,
" I ceaseless verdure boast;
Ever green I appear, in the noon of the year,
Ever green in the winter's frost!

" The brightest hues that the rose suffuse,
Know but a transient reign;
And when *their* bloom hath found a tomb,
Mine, fadeless doth remain!"

" I do not sigh that I early die,"
    Meekly the Rose replied ;
" Though its glow be brief, yet doth my leaf
    Cast incense, far and wide.

" On the sick man's brow on pillow low,
    My fragrant sweets I shed ;
And the moistened air I perfume where
    Rests the pure infant's head !"

Oh, blessed flower !   A nobler dower
    Hath Heaven vouchsafed to thee,
Than laurels own, though they alone
    In constant verdure be.

In *thy* brief life, with fragrance rife,
    More holiness hath birth,
Than in what lives for years, but gives
    No perfume to the Earth !

THE CROSS.

OH Cross ! The time has been thy name
Was synonyme for vilest shame ;
Then was it written, " *on the Tree
Whoso shall hang accurs'd is he.*"

Unto the Cross the scornful Jews
Conduct the Saviour they refuse ;
Upon the Cross his form suspend,
His days with infamy to end.

But centuries thence the Cross was worn
On knightly robes, the Cross was borne
On regal banners ; rallying cry,
" THE CROSS"—of Europe's Chivalry.

When young and noble in our days,
On their ancestral scutcheons gaze,
With pride they hail the Cross, the sign
That seals the honour of their line.

Blessed Redeemer ! Things most base
Failed to taint *thee* with their disgrace,
In thy full glory lost their shame,
And *sacred*—to the World became.

———

TINTERN ABBEY.

IT was a day in summer when mine eye,
Dear Abbey, on thine ancient walls did rest,
Roofless, save for the ceiling of the sky.
Harmonious contrast !—It befits thee best.

Sacred to Time ! For thee methinks the Past,
Her memory to perpetuate, did devise ;—
A record that should long her life outlast,
And win her tears from the sad Future's eyes.

And as thou standest mantled by the leaves
Of the green plants which all around thee twine,
My Fancy thee a hoary sage conceives,
Worshipp'd by far descendants of his line.

The dead beneath thee!—I could almost wait
To see them rise by yonder column dim—
Their chiefs resume their sacerdotal state,
And ere the twilight raise their Vesper hymn.

And sad it seems, that they who here held sway
Should sleep beneath a now unlettered stone;
Fates of their humbler brethren in their day,
Watched, flattered, honoured, knelt to—and unknown!

Little the Abbot deemed at eventide,
As slowly wended he through gardens fair,
With portly mien and movement dignified,
His awful name should be unreverenced there.

The Friar who followed him with decent awe,
And knew no greater on the earth than he,
Never perchance the coming hour foresaw,
When Lord and Monk alike unrecked should be.

Me musing thus—from reverie awoke
The old Custodian of the sacred pile;
Harshly upon mine ear his accents broke;
I turned, and bade him cease his tale awhile.

Another moment, and the ancient mien
Of that old servitor engaged my thought;
His thin, grey hair, bowed frame, yet look serene,
Were in accordance with the tranquil spot.

" Here," said I, " is God's Temple in decay,
A scene sublimer than the Ruin hoar,
When its last vestige shall have passed away,
Its very being unremembered more—

" This failing Human Edifice may Heaven
With beauty greater than its past endow;
By Time untouched, by hostile force unriven,
No change that Home of Spirit then shall know!"

And then methought—ah, would that they, whose eyes
Seek in fragmental stone for the sublime;
Would learn its nobler instances to prize
In those whose destinies are not of Time!

THE LITTLE TOWN.

WITHIN the limits of our isle
   A little town I know;
Its memory sometimes moves a smile,
   And sometimes wakens woe.

The honours due to ancient years
   Scarce to that town belong;
Nor boasts it aught that Fame endears,
   Or consecrates by Song.

Yet unlike towns of modern date
   By Fashion's votaries sought—
Lovers of concert, ball, or fête,
   Do never there resort.

The noise of traffic is unknown
   Within its thoroughfare;
And still Retirement's placid tone
   Is likewise stranger, there.

But through its quaint and narrow streets,
　Dim with perpetual shade—
The slim and formal figure flits
　Of many an ancient maid,

And veteran beaux, who, day by day,
　Meet in the self-same walk,
The vapid noon to while away
　In an insipid talk.

At dusk, Sedans with use outworn,
　Along the narrow way
Salute the eye; *within* are borne
　Like trophies of Decay—

Decay which all high aims doth blight
　That in the heart exist;
Permitting life, two hours each night,
　At the accustomed whist.

For those who round that table throng,
　No other good remains;
They care not for the Poet's song,
　Nor heed the Minstrel's strains!

The names of Heroes in their eyes
　No hues of glory wear;
The Patriot's honoured obsequies
　Ne'er claimed from them, a tear!

The wild flowers rife with perfume sweet,
　They crush with careless tread;
And never they in worship greet
　The planets overhead!

In vain Philosophy displays
  The paths by Sages trod;
In vain Religion points the ways
  That lead the soul to God!

I asked myself—and sad tears found
  Their channel to mine eye—
" Are these my fellow pilgrims, bound
  Unto Eternity?"

LINES

WRITTEN AFTER WITNESSING A RECENT REPRESENTATION
OF "MACBETH" AT DRURY-LANE THEATRE.

TRANSLATOR of the Poet's soul to Sense!
Well did thine art the guilty Thane portray;—
Wakening Ambition's earliest influence,
Vague, shadowy promptings, like to fleet away
Before the holier will;—the dark desire
Whose issue—Crime—did in its womb contain
The sequent sins that must the first maintain;—
And of Remorse, the never dying fire!
But more than all his pinings for that rest
In which unvexed the murdered Duncan lay,—
A lot how happier far than knows the breast,
Though purple robe it, where hid scorpions prey:—
And, 'mid the tumult of approaching strife,
The spell domestic that unnerved his hand
When lapsed from Time, the Spirit darkly grand,—
His Tempter, Doomer, Curse;—but still, his *Wife!*—
Oh! most, this evidence of natural ties
Enduring still,—of holier sympathies

Which in despite of crime, and Virtue's ban,
Despair, and fury—still declared him—*Man*,—
Proclaimed thee meet Interpreter to be,
Of him, whose mind involved Humanity!

May, 1842.

THE OLD TOWER.

The Sage.—What seest thou?

First Spectator.—A pile decayed,
Bricks in cunning fashion laid,
Ruined buttress, moss-clad stone,
Arch with ivy overgrown,
Stairs round which the lichens creep,—
The whole, a desolated heap!

The Sage.—What seest thou?

Second Spectator.—Memorial of olden time,
Telling of the feudal prime,
And the glorious pageantry,
Waking heart, and kindling eye;
And the deep and solemn lore
Learned by hearts that beat no more;
Vows of faith, and high emprise,
Knightly valour, love-lit eyes,
Woman's whisper, trumpet's breath,
Noble daring, valiant death;—
More than History can give
With this ruined tower doth live!

The Sage.—Thus it is that vacant air
MIND informs with visions fair,

Hears its voice's potent sound,
E'en in Silence' self resound,
And all space an echo makes
To the music it awakes!
What are Earth, and Air, and Sea?
Even what thou mak'st them be.
To the Soul whence beauties flow,
Flowers in every desert grow.
Ever signs of sympathy
Meet the sympathetic eye.
To the ear attuned to song
Ceaseless melodies belong.
To a Universal Love
Earth reflects the World above!

THE DEAD.

" Leaves have their time to fall,
   And flowers to wither at the North-Wind's breath ;
And stars to set ;—but all—
   Thou hast all seasons for thine own, Oh, Death !"
                                        MRS. HEMANS.

Go to the high and ancient founts,
   Go to the lonely woods,
Go where the crag-throned chamois mounts,
   Where gush the swelling floods ;
What, though no sculptured stone
   Adorn their lonely bed ;
These spots, where sounds no human tone
   Are peopled with the dead !

The Warrior wounded on the plain,
　　The Pilgrim gray with Time,
The Outcast of the stormy main,
　　Here made themselves a shrine;
The Watchers on their native shore
　　Came forth their bark to hail;
Alas! no wave their vessel bore,
　　No Zephyr swelled their sail!

Ah! well they slumber quietly,
　　And tearless are their eyes;
Their's is the calm serenity,
　　That breathing life denies!
The sighs of agony represt,
　　The tears so often shed,
Are breathed and wept (where'er they rest)
　　Not *by*, but *for* the dead!
1833.

THE RETURN!

It seems to me but yesterday,
　　Since last I left this spot,
And watched the wreathing ivy stray
　　Around this rural cot;
And yet full many a year hath flown,
　　Since on my ear the words
Of loved ones trembled, like the tone
　　Of Summer's fairy birds!

'Twas the still hour of eventide,
　　When here I bade adieu
To each companion, by whose side,
　　To youth my childhood grew!

The faint " God speed ! " the tearful smile,
　　On Memory's page unfurled—
Are present still, as when I hied
　　Away to see the world !

The tones that sound around that hearth,
　　By stranger lips are breathed ;
The chaplet of its evening mirth,
　　By stranger hands is wreathed !
I turn aside—I turn aside—
　　My thoughts roam far away
To those I met that eventide,
　　And ask me, " Where are they ?"

I need not answer—changing years
　　Have rendered answer vain ;
The past, that Memory so endears,
　　She cannot bring again !
I turn aside—I turn aside
　　From Strangers' mirth and glee ;
The home I saw that eventide,
　　Is now no home *for me* !

1833.

HOURS OF EMOTION.

WHEN on the chilly dead
　　Is bent a young child's eye,
And first the bitter lesson read,
　　That all who live must die !

When a loving parent's hand
　　Last rests upon our brow,
And loosed from home, life's cable-band,
　　To sea we turn our prow !

When thoughtless words, unkind,
  The chain of friendship sever;
And tones of pride that zone unbind,
  We should have clasped for ever!

When 'midst the glittering crowd,
  Such parted friends we spy;
And the thoughts the lips have disavowed,
  Are imaged in the eye!

When Sorrow round her brow
  Twines a wreath of short-lived bloom;
When her starting tear-drops flow
  In her own unlighted room!

When a dream at eventide,
  Is thronged with gone-by hours;
And backward seems life's stream to glide,
  To the land of friends and flowers!

When Shade a form assumes,
  And our tearful eyes we cast,
Where Memory's golden torch illumes
  The valley of the past!

When Mercy's hand extends,
  And draws the wounded soul
To Him, that kindest, best of friends,
  Whose love can make it whole!

1833.

TRIBUTARY STANZAS.

Thou art at rest, impassioned child of Love!
Enthusiastic dreamer!   Now no more
Thy joyous presence glads us when we rove
'Midst the dear haunts we visited of yore.

Yet love we well at eventide to stray
Where trees and streams are eloquent of thee;
Where ivied cot, green vale, and turret gray,
Are holy to us by thy memory.

For of the bright and gifted few wert thou,
To whom Creation was no lifeless thing;
O'er its least lovely scenes thy mind could throw
An influence glorious and hallowing.

Thou wert not of the earth—and of thy heart
The language was not read by vulgar eyes;
Then was it well from us thou should'st depart,
Loved one—thy tongue is spoken in the skies !

Daughter of the Ideal! unto thee
This was a strange and unfamiliar land;
And to thee was denied their sympathy,
Who scorned the lore they could not understand.

Then mourn we not for thee, while here thou wert
A light, but making visible the gloom;
Now of the radiant galaxy thou art,
Which gilds with glory thy celestial home!

A RECORD.*

Oh, mournful were our hearts, for we were watchers
    o'er the dying;
Deep silence reigned around—the *look* unto the *look*
    replying;
Profane seemed words, and needless, too; of hand, or
    eye, the sign
Our minds made capable by grief—as language could
    divine!

Our gone-by days came thronging back; each had its
    tale to tell,
Of Benediction and of love;—the workings of the
    spell—
The spell by which all other spells seem weak, if not
    defiled—
The spell which to a Mother binds the being of a Child!

We almost felt her morning kiss as sealed on Child-
    hood's brow;—
Her soft hand parting back the locks that art hath
    braided now;
Almost, we heard her voice dispel the shades of girlish
    care—
And solemn tones preceding ours, at time of evening
    prayer!

---

* These stanzas are intended to record an incident connected
with the departure of a beloved Mother, watched over by her
Children, one of whom wrote the Author an account of the *fact*
alluded to, with a request that he would commemorate it in his verse.

And musing thus, on our beloved we bent our anxious
    eyes,
To find—alas ! that *hers* no more should greet these
    lower skies ;
For aye those orbs were dimmed—and from that once
    so gentle face,
Disease had worn the aspect sweet, we so much loved
    to trace.

No sound we breathed, but all retired in silence from
    the room—
Her cheerful chamber once, but then her temporary
    tomb ;
We quitted it awhile ; but back by secret power were
    led
Again to linger there, and watch the features of the
    dead.

The dead ! A moment doubted we if Death indeed
    were there,
For o'er that pain-worn face had Heaven breathed an
    angelic air,
And smile excelling far in love, all we had seen in life,
When gleams of peace but rarely broke through con-
    stant clouds of strife.

Yes ! as we gazed upon that brow bathed as in light
    serene,
And thought how in our dear one's heart terrific war
    had been ;
We deemed such peaceful look—to us, a telegraph
    whereby
Celestial Warriors signal made, of glorious victory.

We wept not for thy parted smiles, dear Mother ! In
    that *last*,
Was more of Love, and more of Heaven, than in the
    gathered Past ;
We mourned not for thine absent tones ; for more than
    they could speak—
Was uttered in that *living* word engraven on thy
    cheek !

We deemed that in thy latest hour, from thoughts of
    this world free—
Spirits to us invisible, had converse held with thee ;
And for our sakes, thou hadst besought some token
    might be given
Of thine angelical discourse ; and hence that smile from
    Heaven !

We joyed that for our questioning hearts, thy love had
    answer won,
That we might know thou wert with God, and with the
    Blessed Son ;
And with the Holy Spirit—who was strength when
    thou wert weak,
And at that moment wrought in thee—" *though being
    dead to speak !*"

And Thou—Great Architect of Heaven ! If thus the
    ruined pile
Of wasted flesh thou dost restore, and gild it with thy
    smile ;
How beauteous must thy Mansion be, which ne'er was
    built with hands,
But as in First Eternity, a Home of Glory stands !
    11*th October*, 1839.

A FAREWELL.

FAREWELL ! I know that oft the sound
   By careless lips is idly spoken ;
And even when breathed by love profound,
   In faltering speech, and accents broken—
Men oft forget that such a word—
Was ever said, or ever heard ?

May the farewell I utter now,
   Not vainly thus disperse in air ;
But wheresoever thou may'st go—
   Attend thee—an unceasing prayer !
'How bless'd thy lot—did *that* require
No other aid than my desire !

Farewell ! Our springs of happiness
   Rise not from state or scene ;
Whatever these—may'st thou possess
   The fount of joy, *within ;*
And with thee bear to every clime,
A bliss beyond the power of Time.

The Light that kindles in the heart,
   Its radiance shed around—
Something of beauty can impart
   Unto the barren ground
And cause the very bleakest skies
To wear a kindness in thine eyes !

Whate'er is bright can make the sign
    Of that is brighter far;
The natural whispers the divine—
    And Night's most radiant star
Appears to Faith's aspiring will,
Glory—but Glory's *shadow*, still!

Bless'd Influence of holy power,
    That turns e'en grief to gain;
Fair as *the future*—makes *the hour*,
    Hears music in the rain;
Dreams by the fire, of Fairy-land,
And wakes to find it—*close at hand!*

To Him—the Father of us all,
    I would commit thee now;
Few be the saddening shades that fall
    Upon thine open brow,
And every cloud which o'er thee bends,
The veil in which a God descends.

Farewell! I feel these words are weak,
    And not what I would say;
The Soul in Time is doomed to speak
    Through the dull coil of clay.
No speech of Earth can truly tell
The fulness of the heart's farewell!

TO UNA.

Whose lot so drear, it ne'er hath known
A kindly smile, a cheering tone?—
The loneliest live not *all alone*.

Some form of love the darkest fate
Exists to bless, and consecrate;
And none are wholly desolate

While 'midst Time's myriad hearts—*one* heart,
To which their own may all impart
Of care or hope—is set apart,

As was methinks thine own for me,
So rich in love and constancy;
Although I so unworthy be.

It far exceeds my bounded lay,
Thy gentle goodness to convey—
Far more its blessings to repay.

Yet meet it seems, ere I repose
From happy labour, at its close
To tell how much to thee it owes.

How much of love to all mankind,
By thine was cherished in my mind—
One genial soul to *all* doth bind!

And thus, since from love's fountain springs
The Poet's best imaginings,
And union with created things,

I may say in this song of mine,
There doth not live a better line
But owns an influence of thine !

Thou know'st how in our earlier days,
Ere partial friendship hinted bays—
Thy smile did still reward my lays.

And when from kindly voices came
The auguries of worthy fame,
That might hereafter grace our name,

'Twas sweeter still within thine eyes
To mark the tears of pleasure rise—
Fit meed for noblest enterprise.

Now whether live my verse—or die;
'Tis due, and pleasant, thus that I
Its debt to thee should testify.

William Stevens, Printer, Bell Yard, Temple Bar.

Printed in the United States
111190LV00004B/123/A

9 781432 643102